VIRGINIA SOCIAL Studies

People and Places, Then and Now

HOUGHTON MIFFLIN HARCOURT
School Publishers

Series Authors

Dr. Michael J. Berson
Professor
Social Science Education
University of South Florida
Tampa, Florida

Dr. Tyrone C. Howard
Associate Professor
UCLA Graduate School of Education &
   Information Studies
University of California Los Angeles
Los Angeles, California

Sara Shoob
Adjunct Instructor
George Mason University
Retired Social Studies Coordinator
Fairfax County Public Schools

Dr. Cinthia Salinas
Associate Professor
Department of Curriculum and
   Instruction
College of Education
The University of Texas at Austin
Austin, Texas

Virginia Consultants and Reviewers

Aliceyn S. Applewhite
Teacher
Park View Elementary School
Portsmouth, VA

Becky W. Baskerville
Principal
Sutherland Elementary School
Sutherland, Virginia

Deanna Beacham
Weapemeoc
Virginia Indian History Consultant
Mechanicsville, Virginia

Lauren W. Berents
Teacher
Shady Grove Elementary School
Glen Allen, Virginia

Katherine R. Bohn
Teacher
Glen Forest Elementary School
Falls Church, Virginia

Kim Briggs
Teacher
Leesville Road Elementary School
Lynchburg, Virginia

Susan K. Dalton
Teacher
Woodstock Elementary School
Virginia Beach, Virginia

James J. Doran
Teacher
Olive Branch Elementary School
Portsmouth, Virginia

Agnes Dunn
Retired Coordinator for Social Studies
Stafford County Public Schools

Jeanie Hawks
Instructional Technology Specialist
Halifax County Public Schools

Sarah Duncan Hinds
Social Studies Instructional Specialist
Portsmouth Public Schools
Portsmouth, Virginia

Carter H. McIntyre
Teacher
Laurel Meadow Elementary School
Mechanicsville, Virginia

Rebecca Mills
Supervisor of Social Studies
Spotsylvania County Public Schools

Jaime Ratliff
Teacher
Stonewall Elementary School
Clearbrook, Virginia

Tanya Lee Siwik
Teacher
Kings Park Elementary School
Springfield, Virginia

Evelyn Soltes
Title 1
Specialist for School Improvement
Richmond Public Schools
Richmond, Virginia

Andrea Nelson Tavenner
Teacher
Swift Creek Elementary School
Midlothian, Virgina

Kathryn Clawson Watkins
Retired Teacher
Chesterfield County

Cathy H. Whittecar
Teacher
Centerville Elementary School
Virginia Beach, Virginia

Karenne Wood
Monacan
Director
Virginia Indian Heritage Program
Kents Store, Virginia

Printed in the U. S. A.

ISBN-13: 978-0-15-384348-8
ISBN-10: 0-15-384348-9

11 1421 17 16
4500583846

Using Your  Textbook

Dear _____

This year your book is different. You can write in it! It's **interactive**.

TextWork

Look for the green TextWork boxes. Each box will ask you to underline, circle, and draw in your book. And you can write the answers right below the questions! So keep those pencils sharp and markers ready.

Explore!

Sometimes you'll see this symbol **EIP** in your book. It tells you and your teacher where to get more information. You might look at something more closely. You might take a virtual tour or watch a video. Enjoy the Electronic Interactive Presentations (EIP).

Are you ready to use a new kind of textbook? Then let's get started!

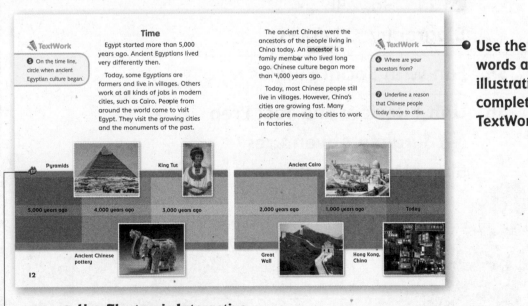

Use the words and illustrations to complete the TextWork.

Use Electronic Interactive Presentations to study and explore content.

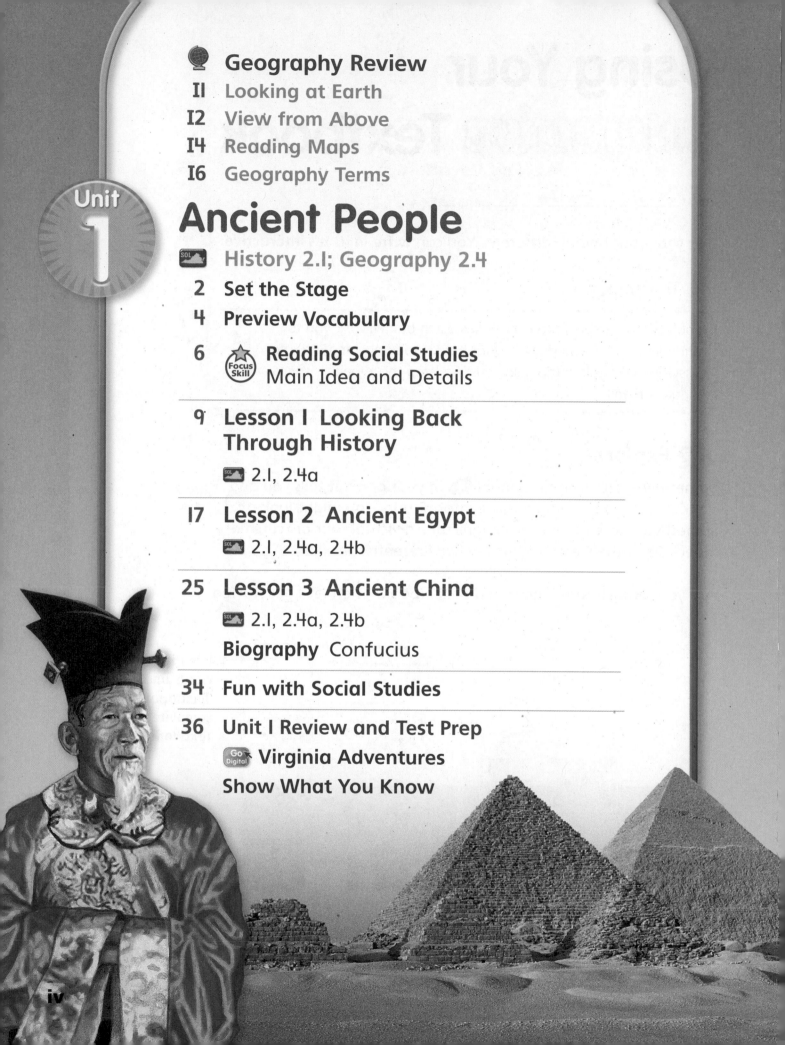

iv

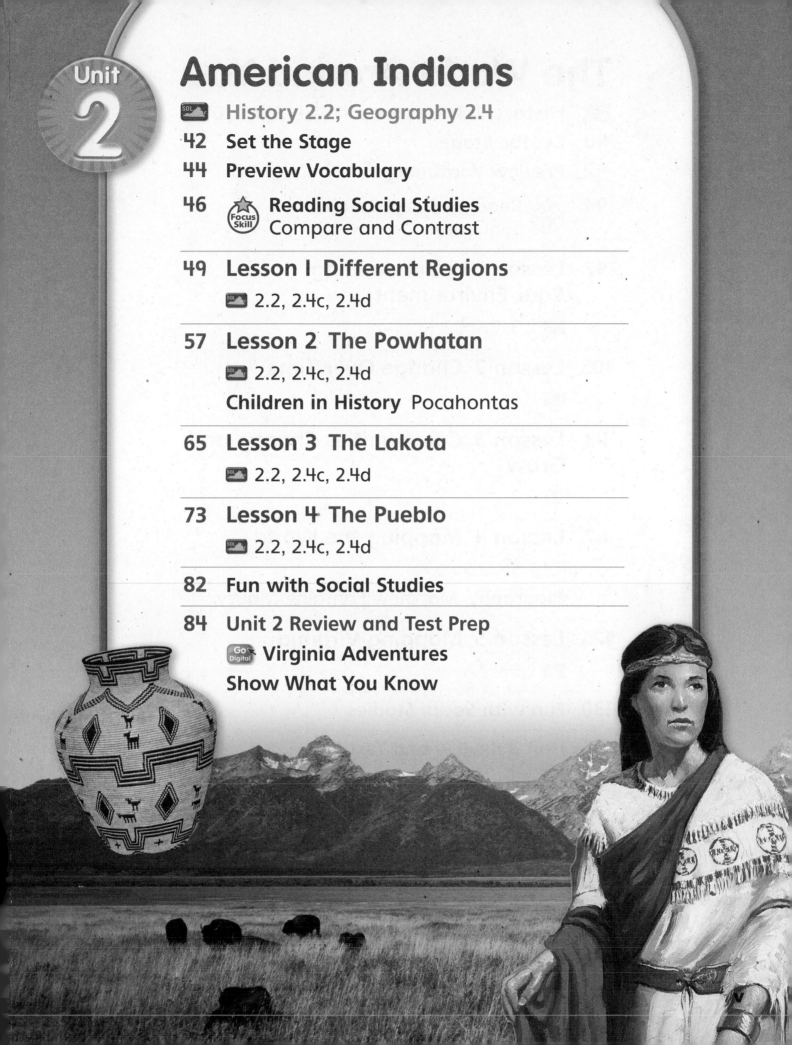

Unit 2

American Indians

History 2.2; Geography 2.4

Unit 3

The World Around You

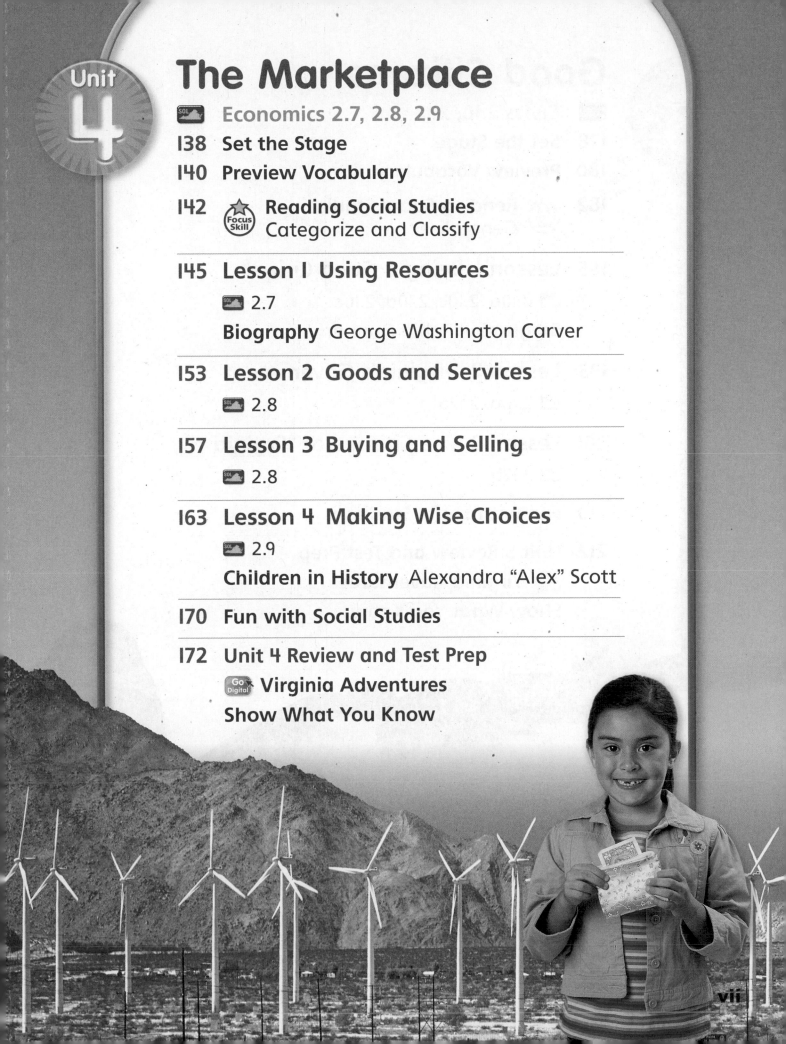

Unit 4

The Marketplace

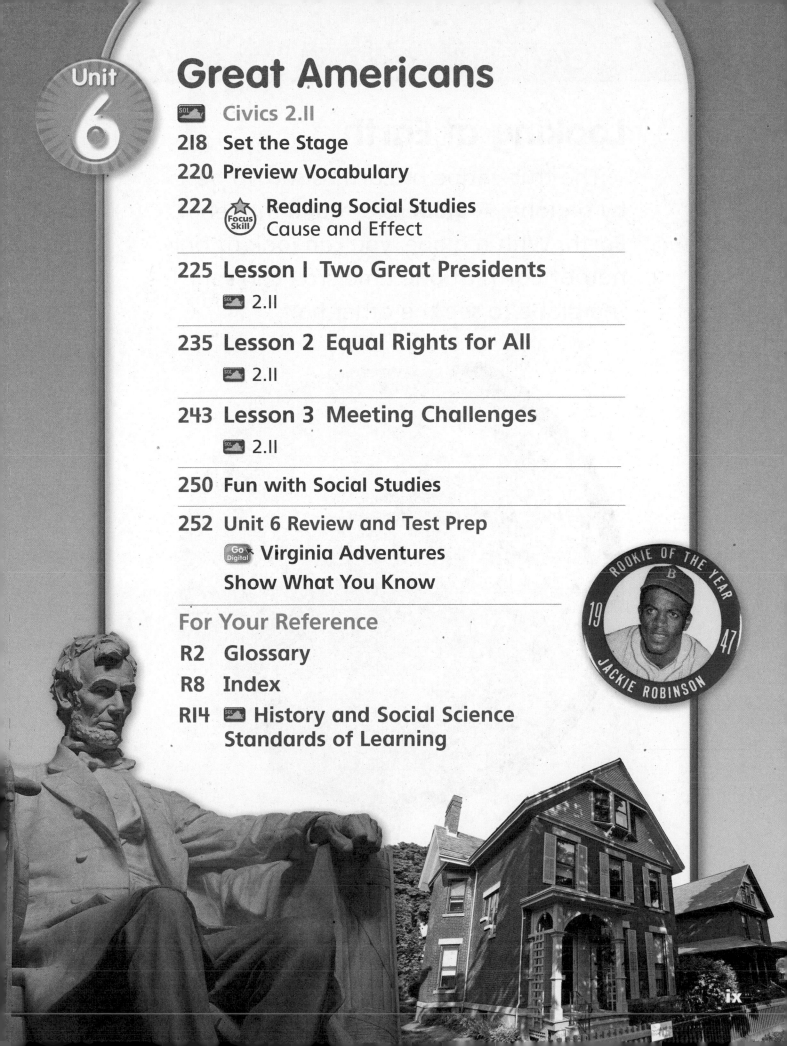

ROOKIE OF THE YEAR
19 47
JACKIE ROBINSON

Looking at Earth

The true shape of Earth is shown best by a globe. A **globe** is a round model of Earth. With a globe, you can look at only half of Earth at one time. You can spin the globe to see the other half.

On a map of the world, you can see all the land and water at once. A **map** is a drawing that shows where places are located. This map shows the seven continents. A **continent** is a large body of land on Earth. This map also shows large areas of water called **oceans**.

Circle the names of the seven continents. Then underline the names of the five oceans you see on this map.

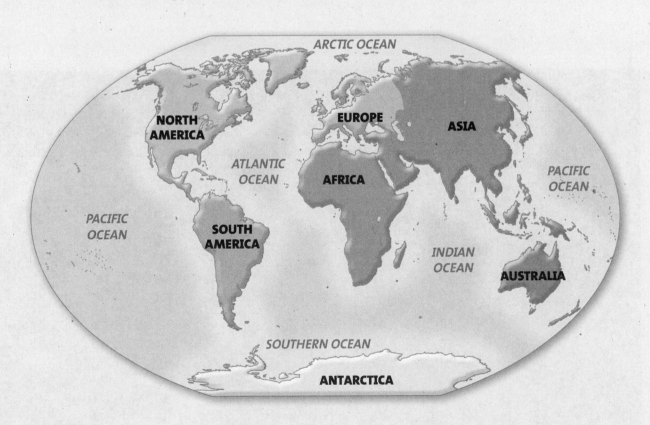

ARCTIC OCEAN

NORTH AMERICA

EUROPE

ASIA

ATLANTIC OCEAN

AFRICA

PACIFIC OCEAN

PACIFIC OCEAN

SOUTH AMERICA

INDIAN OCEAN

AUSTRALIA

SOUTHERN OCEAN

ANTARCTICA

View from Above

Does your neighborhood have a school, a grocery store, a library, a fire station, a park, and a bank? These are places that people share in a neighborhood. You can learn about a neighborhood by looking at a photograph.

You can also learn about a neighborhood by looking at a map. Mapmakers use photographs taken from above to draw maps.

How is this map like the photograph? How is it different?

_____

_____

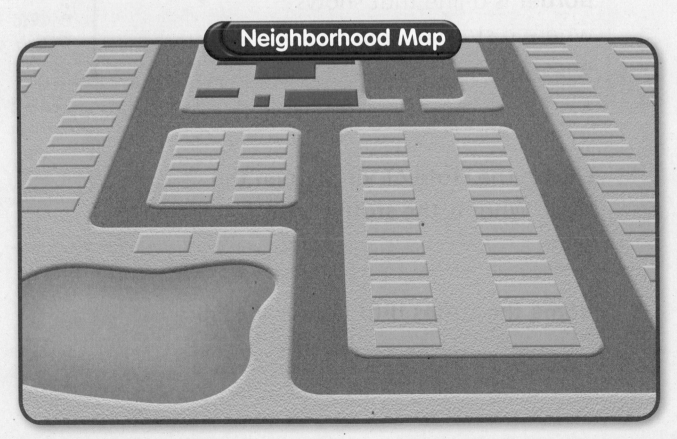

Neighborhood Map

Reading Maps

Maps are used to show many different kinds of information. This is a map of our country, the United States. A **country** is an area of land with its own people and laws. On this map, you can find all the **states** that are part of the United States. You can also find each state's borders. A **border** is a line that shows where a state or country ends.

ARCTIC OCEAN

ALASKA

CANADA

Juneau★

PACIFIC OCEAN

WASHINGTON

Olympia★

Salem★

OREGON

Carson City

Sacramento★

CALIFORNIA

PACIFIC OCEAN

HAWAII

Honolulu★

PACIFIC OCEAN

Locate the state of Virginia on the map. What is the state capital?

_____

Name the states that border Virginia.

_____

_____

Check the **map title** to see what area is being shown.

The United States

A compass rose shows directions. The **cardinal directions** are north, south, east, and west.

Map Legend
⊛ National capital
★ State capital
— Border

A **map symbol** is a small picture or shape that stands for a real thing.

desert a large, dry area of land

forest a large area of land covered with trees

gulf a large body of ocean water that is partly surrounded by land

hill a landform that rises above the land around it

island land with water all around it

lake a body of water with land all around it

mountain highest kind of landform

ocean a body of salt water that covers a large area

peninsula land that is almost completely surrounded by water

plain flat land

river a large stream of water that flows across the land

valley low land between hills or mountains

16

Ancient People

Pyramid of Khafre

Spotlight on Standards

THE BIG IDEA The ancient Egyptians and the ancient Chinese made contributions that affect today's world.

HISTORY AND SOCIAL SCIENCE SOL
2.1, 2.4a, 2.4b

1

Set the Stage

How did people who lived long ago affect our lives today?

"Some of the world's first clocks were made in Egypt."

2

恭
禧
發
財

" Silk cloth was first made in
China thousands of years ago."

"The Chinese invented
the compass."

3

Preview Vocabulary

ancient

People who lived in **ancient** times made objects that we can study. (page 10)

culture

My family and I wear special clothes that show our **culture**. (page 10)

contribution

The ancient Chinese made a **contribution** to writing and printing. (page 20)

architecture

Pyramids are an example of ancient Egyptian **architecture**. (page 23)

invention

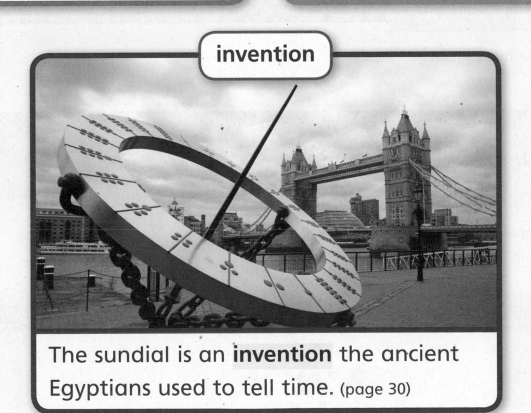

The sundial is an **invention** the ancient Egyptians used to tell time. (page 30)

Main Idea and Details

Learn

- The main idea tells you what you are reading about. It is the most important idea.

- The details explain the main idea.

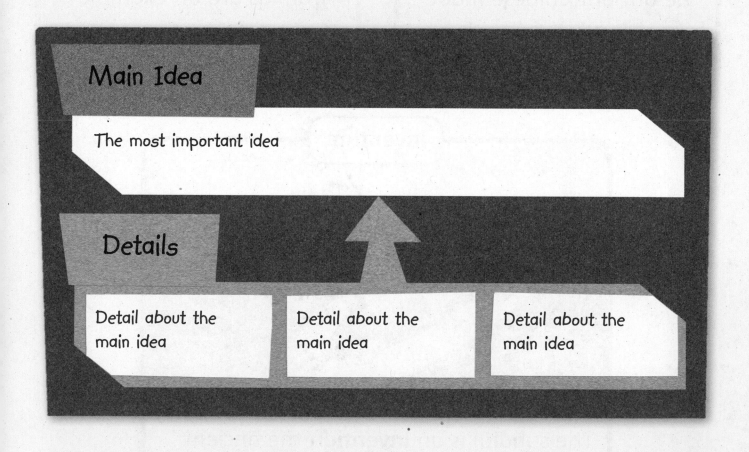

Main Idea

The most important idea

Details

Detail about the main idea

Detail about the main idea

Detail about the main idea

Practice

Underline one detail in the paragraph.

The pharaoh Tutankhamen is often called The Boy King. As a child, Tutankhamen probably spent his time playing games, swimming, and studying. When his father died, Tutankhamen became the leader of Egypt. He was only eight years old. With the help of adults, he ruled his country for ten years.

Main Idea

Detail

The Boy King

Apply

Read the following paragraph.

In 1922, a scientist discovered Tutankhamen's tomb, or the place where he was buried. Many treasures were found in the tomb. Some were precious stones and jewels. The young king's funeral mask was made from solid gold! Scientists also found everyday objects, such as furniture, lamps, jars, and games.

What details about Tutankhamen's tomb can you add to the chart below?

Main Idea

Tutankhamen's tomb was discovered by a scientist in 1922.

Details

Many treasures were found in the tomb.

_____

_____

_____

_____

Looking Back Through History

Lesson 1

Think about what places were like long, long ago.

Essential Questions
✓ What examples of architecture from ancient Egypt and China are still present today?
✓ Where are Egypt and China located on a world map?

 HISTORY AND SOCIAL SCIENCE SOL
2.1, 2.4a

9

Long, Long Ago

Since **ancient** times, or times very long ago, people have lived in groups. Over time, people in these groups developed their own **culture**, or way of life. Food, clothes, art, music, and beliefs are all parts of a group's culture.

![TextWork icon] **TextWork**

❶ What is another word that means very long ago?

_____

❷ Circle the picture that shows a culture's art.

We can study ancient artifacts. An artifact is an object that was used by people in the past.

We can learn about ancient cultures from things people made and stories they told. Folktales, artifacts, and buildings tell about a culture's **history**, or the story of what happened in the past.

In this unit, you will learn about two ancient cultures, Egypt and China. People still live in these countries today, but the way they live has changed over time.

TextWork

❸ (Focus Skill) Underline some things that tell about a culture's history.

❹ In the picture, circle some ways life has changed in China.

Shanghai, China

11

Time

TextWork

5 On the time line, circle when ancient Egyptian culture began.

Egypt started more than 5,000 years ago. Ancient Egyptians lived very differently then.

Today, some Egyptians are farmers and live in villages. Others work at all kinds of jobs in modern cities, such as Cairo. People from around the world come to visit Egypt. They visit the growing cities and the monuments of the past.

Pyramids

King Tut

5,000 years ago

4,000 years ago

3,000 years ago

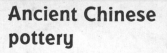

Ancient Chinese pottery

12

The ancient Chinese were the ancestors of the people living in China today. An **ancestor** is a family member who lived long ago. Chinese culture began more than 4,000 years ago.

Today, most Chinese people still live in villages. However, China's cities are growing fast. Many people are moving to cities to work in factories.

TextWork

6 Where are your ancestors from?

_____

7 Underline a reason that Chinese people today move to cities.

Ancient Cairo

2,000 years ago   **1,000 years ago**   **Today**

Great Wall

Hong Kong, China

Place

Ancient Egypt started along the Nile River in Africa. The Nile is the longest river in the world. It flows north through Egypt into the Mediterranean Sea. The land near the Nile is good for growing crops.

In the southern part of Egypt is the Sahara, the largest desert in the world. A **desert** is a large, dry area of land. The Sahara stretches from Egypt to the Atlantic Ocean.

TextWork

8 Label Egypt on the globe.

9 (Focus Skill) What kind of land does most of Egypt have?

_____

Sahara

Nile River

China is a very large country in Asia. China has hills, valleys, and deserts. It also has some of the world's longest rivers and highest mountains.

Places in the north of China get very cold. Places in the south are usually warm. Places near the ocean get lots of rain. Winds called monsoons change the weather. In different seasons, they blow dry air or wet air across China.

 **TextWork**

10 Why does China have so many different kinds of weather?

_____

_____

_____

Li River

Mustagh Ata Mountain

Lesson 1 Review

1 **SUMMARIZE** On which continents are Egypt and China located?

_____

_____

2 How can we learn about a group's **history**?

_____

_____

Circle the letter of the correct answer.

3 Where is the land in Egypt good for growing crops?

   A Near the Mediterranean Sea

   B In the Sahara

   C Near the Nile River

   D In the mountains

Activity

Draw a kind of land or water in Egypt and China. Add your drawings to a class scrapbook as you study more.

16

Ancient Egypt

Great Sphinx

Think about what you might learn from things made long ago.

Essential Questions

✓ How did the environment affect the culture of Egypt?
✓ How did the ancient Egyptians relate to their environment?
✓ What inventions came from ancient Egypt?
✓ What contributions did the people of ancient Egypt make to the development of written language?
✓ What examples of architecture from ancient Egypt are still present today?

 HISTORY AND SOCIAL SCIENCE SOL
2.1, 2.4a, 2.4b

17

Life in Ancient Egypt

Most ancient Egyptians were farmers. They grew wheat, barley, and flax. They used water from the Nile River to water their crops. The Egyptians hunted and fished. They traded to get things they needed.

The ancient Egyptians built homes from mud brick. The homes were painted white to reflect the hot sun. They had small windows high up on the walls to keep out the dust.

18

Some Egyptians worked as builders or priests. Others were craftworkers who made baskets, pottery, and jewelry. Egyptian doctors made medicines from plants, treated wounds, and set broken bones.

The Egyptians were ruled by powerful kings called pharaohs. In times of war, pharaohs were in charge of the army. Egyptian soldiers rode on chariots, or two-wheeled carts pulled by horses.

❷ ⭐(Focus Skill) Underline some jobs of Egyptian doctors.

❸ How did chariots help soldiers?

_____

_____

_____

Egyptian Contributions

The ancient Egyptians made many contributions to the ways people lived. A **contribution** is the sharing of a new idea for doing something. People have learned a lot from the ancient Egyptians' contributions.

The early Egyptians figured out ways to tell the time. They used shadow clocks to track the time of day. They knew it was noon when the shadow was the shortest.

❹ How did Egyptians use the shadow clock to tell it was noon?

_____

_____

Visitors look at a sundial at the Library of Alexandria in Egypt.

20

One of the first calendars with 365 days was made in ancient Egypt. A **calendar** is a chart of the days, weeks, and months in a year.

Egyptian scientists saw something important in the sky. They saw that a very bright star would rise next to the sun every 365 days. That was around the time when the Nile River began flooding its banks each year. The Egyptians made their calendar based on that star and the sun.

TextWork

5 What happened in Egypt each year?

_____

_____

The Egyptians carved this calendar on the walls of a temple.

6 Underline the sentence that explains hieroglyphics.

7 How did the Egyptians use papyrus reeds?

_____

_____

Written Language

We know Egyptian history from ancient writings. Writers called **scribes** carved symbols into stone. These symbols, or hieroglyphics, were pictures that stood for sounds. Scientists can read the hieroglyphics carved on ancient Egyptian walls.

Egyptians made a kind of paper out of papyrus reeds. They wrote with reed pens and ink.

Our word paper comes from the word papyrus.

Architecture

One of the greatest contributions of ancient Egyptians is their architecture. **Architecture** is the design of buildings. Hundreds of workers moved tons of stone to build temples, statues, and tombs.

The pyramids were built as giant tombs for the Egyptian pharaohs. Food and treasures were buried with the pharaoh for the dead leader to use in the afterlife.

TextWork

❽ What was buried inside the pyramids?

_____

Pyramids of Giza

① SUMMARIZE What Egyptian contributions do we use in our lives today?

_____

_____

② Name an example of ancient Egyptian architecture that can still be seen today.

_____

Circle the letter of the correct answer.

③ How did the ancient Egyptians honor their pharaohs?

    A They planted crops.

    B They built pyramids.

    C They went to war.

    D They made calendars.

Activity

Create your own picture writing. Think of a symbol to stand for each letter of your first name. Then write your name, using those symbols.

Ancient China

Lesson **3**

Think of a time when you watched a fireworks show.

Downtown Guiyang, China

Essential Questions

✔ How did the environment affect the culture of China?
✔ How did the ancient Chinese relate to their environment?
✔ What inventions came from ancient China?
✔ What contributions did the people of ancient China make to the development of written language?
✔ What examples of architecture from ancient China are still present today?

 HISTORY AND SOCIAL SCIENCE SOL
2.1, 2.4a, 2.4b

25

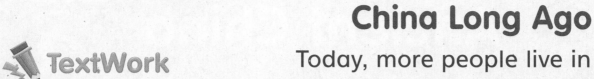
❶ Underline the meaning of the word civilization.

China Long Ago

Today, more people live in China than in any other country. China is one of the oldest civilizations in the world. A **civilization** is a large group of people living in a well-organized way. The ancient Chinese had strong leaders. They built cities and highways. They made beautiful works of art.

For thousands of years, the people of China were separated from other people. The oceans, mountains, and deserts that border China made travel hard. Because of this, the Chinese kept their own ways of life.

The people in ancient China were like other ancient people in some ways. They were farmers, fishers, builders, and traders. They made new and better tools and passed on new ideas.

TextWork

2 Circle what separated China from the rest of the world.

3 🌟 Underline some of the jobs of the ancient Chinese.

Working the Land

Because China is such a large country, it has many different kinds of land, or landforms. Among these are great forests, long rivers, and wide deserts.

Much of the land is too hilly or too dry for growing the large amounts of food needed. The ancient Chinese used technology to solve this problem. **Technology** is the use of new objects and ideas to make everyday life better.

TextWork

❹ Why was it hard for farmers to grow large amounts of food?

_____

_____

_____

28

The ancient Chinese settled in places that were good for farming, such as along the banks of the Huang He. Farmers learned to grow crops on hills by building terraces. Terraces are flat ledges cut into hillsides. Canals brought water from rivers to the terraces.

Some Chinese farmers raised silkworms. Weavers made cloth from the silk thread gathered from the cocoons. For many years, silk cloth was made only in China.

29

Chinese Inventions

The ancient Chinese made many inventions to improve their daily lives. An **invention** is something that has not been made before.

🖍 **TextWork**

7 Circle the invention that helped the ancient Chinese find directions.

The Chinese floated magnets in water to make compasses.

Bronze was used to make cooking pots, tools, and weapons.

The Chinese made gunpowder and used it for fireworks to scare off their enemies.

Kites were first used to measure distances to enemy camps.

30

Written Language

Like the Egyptians, the Chinese use picture characters in their writing. Each one stands for a sound or an idea. Written Chinese has about 3,000 characters!

The Chinese invented paper and printing. First, they made a mash of bits of wood and water. They rolled it out and dried it in the sun to make paper. Later, they rubbed wooden blocks with ink and used them to print on the paper.

Biography

Fairness

Confucius EIP

Confucius was a wise man who lived in China more than 2,500 years ago. He believed that you should always treat others the way you want to be treated. Confucius's teachings were later written in books. People still follow many of his teachings today.

❾ What was the Great Wall used for?

_____

_____

Architecture

One of the most lasting Chinese contributions to architecture is the Great Wall. It was started more than 2,000 years ago to protect China from its enemies.

Builders added to the Great Wall over time until it stretched about 4,000 miles. In some places, it is as high as 32 feet. It was made wide enough for people to walk or even ride horses on top.

Great Wall of China

1 SUMMARIZE What contributions made by the people of ancient China affect the way we live today?

_____

_____

2 What is one ancient Chinese **invention** that we still use today?

_____

Circle the letter of the correct answer.

3 The ancient Chinese changed the land to help them grow crops by—

   A building terraces
   B flattening hills
   C building fences
   D digging wells

Writing

Research one of the Chinese inventions from this lesson. Write a paragraph explaining how it has changed over time.

Ancient Cultures
Tic-Tac-Toe

Find and circle three items in a row that were invented by the same culture.

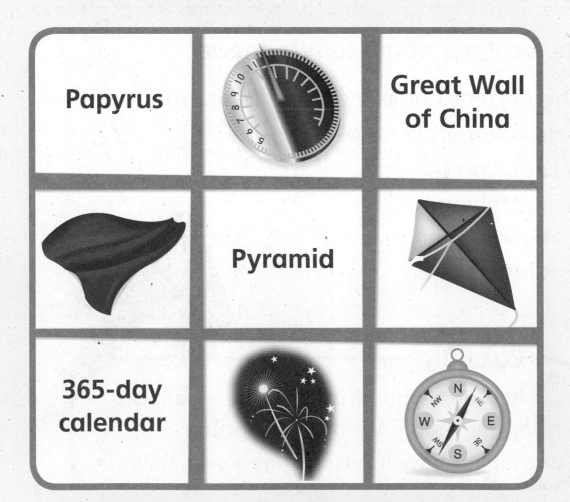

Papyrus		Great Wall of China
	Pyramid	
365-day calendar		

Vacation Station

What country does each vacation poster advertise?

_____

Mountains, deserts, rivers, and a big wall— this country has it all!

_____

The Nile will make you smile!

Review and Test Prep

The Big Idea

The ancient Egyptians and the ancient Chinese made contributions that affect today's world.

Summarize the Unit

Focus Skill Main Idea and Details Fill in the graphic organizer to show some contributions of ancient people.

Main Idea

The ancient Egyptians and the ancient Chinese made contributions to writing, architecture, and technology.

Details

papyrus paper, printing

_____

_____

_____

_____

_____

_____

Use Vocabulary

Fill in the blanks with the correct words.

People lived in Egypt and China in

1 _____ times. They made

many **2** _____ to the way

we live today. They made many new

3 _____, such as calendars,

kites, and paper. They also created great

works of **4** _____, such

as the pyramids and the Great Wall of
China. These things show each group's

5 _____, or way of living.

> ### Word Bank
>
> **ancient**
> p. 10
>
> **culture**
> p. 10
>
> **contributions**
> p. 20
>
> **architecture**
> p. 23
>
> **civilization**
> p. 26
>
> **inventions**
> p. 30

Think About It

Circle the letter of the correct answer.

6 Which word comes from the Egyptian word <u>papyrus</u>?

  A Calendar

  B Paper

  C Scribe

  D History

7 Which group lived along the banks of the Nile River?

  F Egyptians

  G Chinese

  H Africans

  J Americans

8 To scare their enemies, the ancient Chinese used—

  A fireworks

  B compasses

  C kites

  D clocks

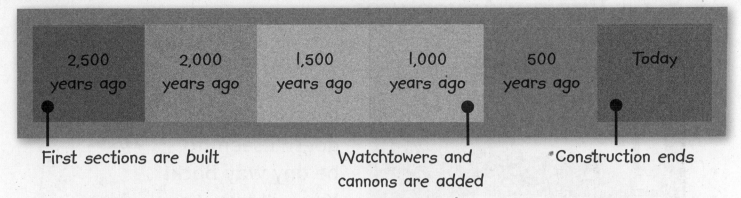

2,500 years ago   2,000 years ago   1,500 years ago   1,000 years ago   500 years ago   Today

First sections are built

Watchtowers and cannons are added

Construction ends

What happened about 350 years ago?

F The building of the Great Wall began.

G Watchtowers and cannons were added.

H Kites and fireworks signaled the end of war.

J The building of the Great Wall was finished.

Answer each question in a complete sentence.

⑩ Why do you think Egyptian pharaohs were buried with food and treasure?

_____

_____

⑪ Explain why the Chinese invention of printing with wood blocks was important.

_____

_____

Virginia Adventures

What are we doing in ancient Egypt...?

Eco has fallen down the time line, and there doesn't seem to be any way back! You will travel to ancient Egypt and China to search for Eco. Play the game now, online or on CD.

Show What You Know

Writing Write a Help Wanted Ad
Choose one job the ancient Egyptians did and write an advertisement for the job. Include the job duties in the description.

Activity Draw a Picture
Ancient people made many inventions to help them with their daily lives. Draw a picture of an invention you would like to make to help people.

American Indians

Powhatan Indian Village,
Jamestown Settlement

Spotlight on Standards

THE BIG IDEA American Indians have lived in Virginia and in other regions of North America for thousands of years.

HISTORY AND SOCIAL SCIENCE SOL
2.2, 2.4c, 2.4d

41

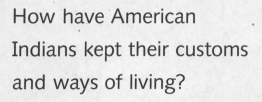

Set the Stage

How have American Indians kept their customs and ways of living?

"American Indians used the resources around them to make the things they used every day."

42

Lakota in traditional dress

"American Indians dress in traditional clothing on special days."

"American Indians have passed down their stories and songs."

Pueblo Tales

Preview Vocabulary

environment

We must take care of our **environment**.
(page 50)

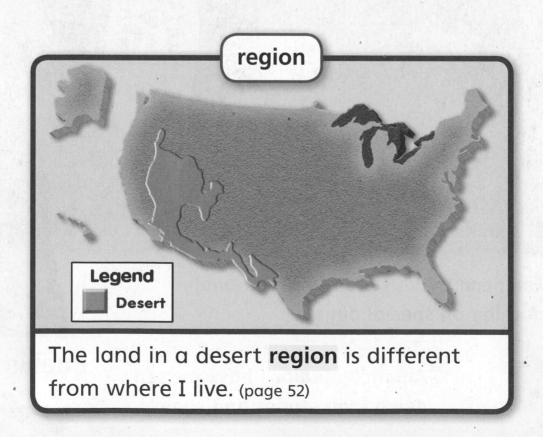

region

Legend
▢ Desert

The land in a desert **region** is different from where I live. (page 52)

climate

This part of the world has a very cold **climate**. (page 52)

dugout

The Powhatan made **dugouts** from large tree trunks. (page 60)

adobe

The Pueblo built their homes from **adobe**. (page 75)

Focus Skill

Compare and Contrast

Learn

■ To compare, think about how people, places, or things are alike.

■ To contrast, think about how they are different.

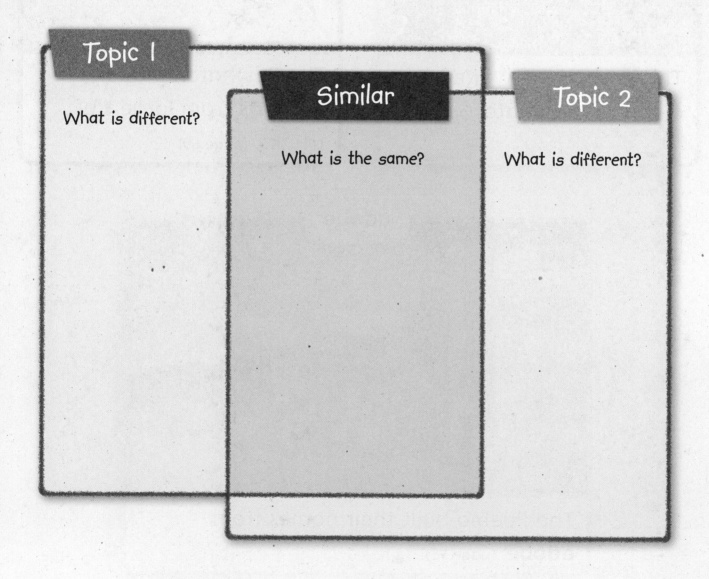

Practice

Read the paragraph below. Underline the sentence that tells what is the same about American Indians long ago and today.

Long ago, American Indians lived in different areas of what is now the United States. They farmed the land and hunted animals. Today, many American Indians live on reservations. They work in all kinds of jobs. Like they did long ago, American Indians still follow their beliefs and traditions.

Topic 1

Topic 2

Long Ago

Pamunkey Chief
Opechancanough

Today

Pamunkey Chief
William Miles

Apply

Read the following paragraph.

Long ago, the Pamunkey were part of the Powhatan Confederacy. They fished in the Pamunkey River and hunted in the forests. Both long ago and today, they work to protect their culture and resources. Today, the Pamunkey live on the reservation or in nearby cities. The reservation's museum shows their history and arts. The Pamunkey also raise and release millions of shad fish back into the wild.

What can you add to the chart?

Pamunkey long ago	Similar	Pamunkey today
were part of the Powhatan Confederacy	work to protect their culture and resources	live on a reservation and in nearby cities
_____	_____	_____
_____	_____	_____
_____	_____	_____

Imagine how the land and water around you looked five hundred years ago.

Essential Questions

✔ Where are the regions of the Powhatan, Lakota, and Pueblo people located on a United States map?

✔ How did the environment affect the Powhatan, Lakota, and Pueblo Indians?

✔ In what ways were past American Indian lifestyles in Virginia similar to and different from those of the Lakota and Pueblo Indians?

HISTORY AND SOCIAL SCIENCE SOL
2.2, 2.4c, 2.4d

49

1 Who were the first people to live in North America?

_____

Early North Americans

American Indians were the first people to live in North America. They have lived there for many thousands of years. Many different groups lived in different places. Each American Indian group had its own culture. Members of each group used their **environment**, or surroundings, to meet their needs.

50

American Indians knew how to find and grow food. They hunted animals for food and used the skins for clothing. Some groups built homes from wood, while others used earth.

Today, some American Indians still live in their homelands. Others live and work in cities all over the United States. Many have kept their cultures.

TextWork

2 **Focus Skill** Circle the ways American Indian groups were alike.

Today

Long ago

3 Underline the sentence that explains the word climate.

4 Look at the map. What large body of water borders the Eastern Woodlands?

_____

American Indian Lands

Three American Indian groups in North America were the Powhatan, the Lakota, and the Pueblo. The map shows the regions where each group lived. A **region** is an area of land with common features.

Each region has its own land, bodies of water, and climate. **Climate** is the kind of weather a place has over a long time. A region's land and climate affected the way American Indians lived.

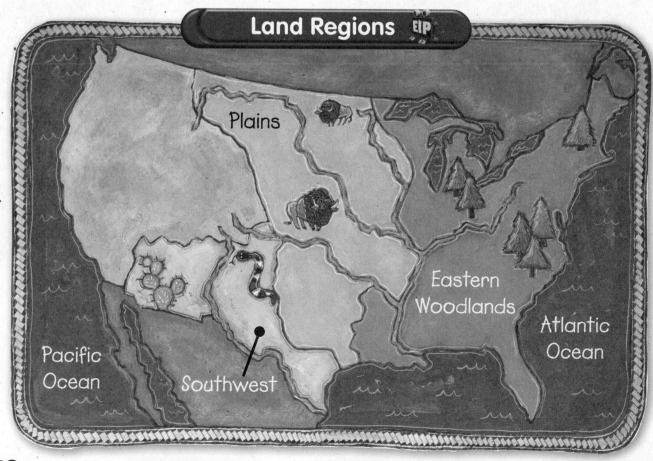

Land Regions EIP

Plains

Eastern Woodlands

Atlantic Ocean

Pacific Ocean

Southwest

The Eastern Woodlands

The Powhatan lived in the Eastern Woodlands. This region has many forests, rivers, and streams. It has mild winters and hot summers.

The Powhatan and other Woodland groups used wood from the forests to make homes and tools. They grew corn and other vegetables. They ate fruits and nuts that grew on trees. They also hunted the animals that lived in the forests.

5 What did American Indians get from forests?

_____

_____

James River in Virginia

The Plains

✏️ **TextWork**

6 🔵 How were the people of the Eastern Woodlands and the people of the Plains similar?

_____

_____

The Lakota live on the Plains. A **plain** is a large area of land that is mostly flat. The Plains are covered in grasses. This region has hot summers and very cold winters.

American Indians who lived on the Plains followed and hunted herds of buffalo. From the buffalo, they got meat to eat and hides to make clothing and shelters. They also gathered wild plants for food.

Buffalo were very important to the Lakota.

The Southwest

The Pueblo people live in the desert Southwest. Days in the desert can get very hot, while nights can be freezing cold.

Even though the desert is very dry, the American Indians who lived there learned to grow crops. They learned how to store water and food for hard times.

**TextWork**

7 Underline the words that describe the climate in the desert.

The Southwest has many cliffs, canyons, and mountains.

1 SUMMARIZE How are the Eastern Woodlands and the Southwest regions different?

_____

_____

_____

2 In which **region** did the Powhatan live?

_____

Circle the letter of the correct answer.

3 Which sentence describes the Southwest?

　A It has mild winters and hot summers.

　B Its land is covered in grasses.

　C It has many rivers and streams.

　D It has a very dry climate.

Activity

　Find out more about the three regions in this lesson. Draw pictures of the kinds of land and water in each region.

The Powhatan

Think about how your life would be different as a Powhatan long ago.

Powhatan Indian Village, Jamestown Settlement

Essential Questions

✓ How did the Powhatan relate to their environment?
✓ What are some contributions of American Indian culture to present-day life?

 HISTORY AND SOCIAL SCIENCE SOL
2.2, 2.4c, 2.4d

Early America

For thousands of years, American Indian groups have lived in what is today Virginia. One group was the Powhatan. They lived in eastern Virginia, near the coast. Today, some American Indians still live in these areas.

The Powhatan built their towns near rivers, bays, or other bodies of water. Some towns were small. Others had as many as 100 homes.

TextWork

1 Circle the words that tell where the Powhatan built their towns.

Wall for protection

Powhatan Ways of Life

Houses built from trees and bark

Making a dugout canoe

58

Powhatan Homes

The Powhatan built oval-shaped homes. Today, these buildings are sometimes called longhouses. The Powhatan bent small trees and tied them together. Then, they covered the trees with reed mats or tree bark. At each end of the longhouse was an opening covered by a reed mat or animal skin. In the middle of the longhouse was a fire for cooking food. An opening at the top let out the smoke.

TextWork

2 Circle the things used to make a longhouse.

3 In the picture, why do you think there is a wall around the town?

_____

_____

Hunting animals for food

Farming in fields

Travel and Trade

The Powhatan made many paths through the woods for walking to neighboring towns. They also used dugout canoes to travel on rivers. A **dugout** is a boat made from a large, hollowed-out tree trunk. Some canoes were 50 feet long!

The Powhatan traded with other American Indian groups for items they could not make or grow. They traded dried oysters and shells for furs and copper.

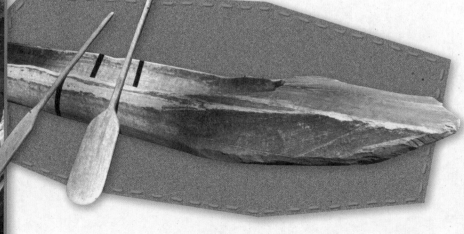

The Powhatan burned the inside of tree trunks to make them into canoes.

60

Fishing and Hunting

Powhatan men fished in the rivers and streams. They caught the fish by using spears or nets. They also dug clams and gathered oysters near the shore.

The men hunted deer, beavers, and turkeys in the forests. They used bows and arrows, spears, and traps to hunt. These weapons were made from wood, shells, stone, and animal bones.

5 Underline the animals the Powhatan fished for and hunted.

6 Which part of a weapon might be made from stone?

_____

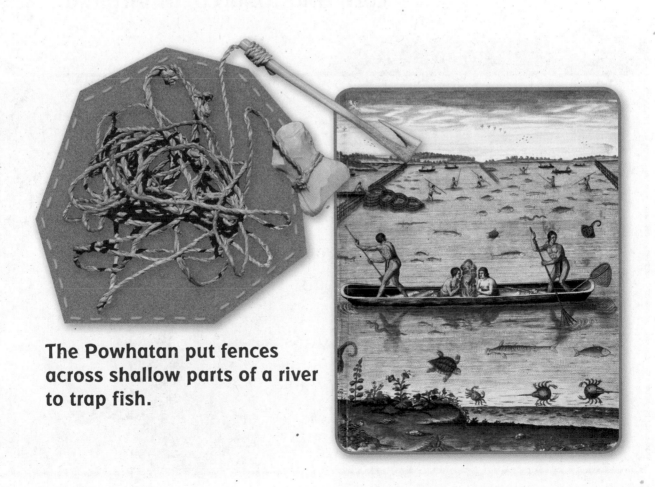

The Powhatan put fences across shallow parts of a river to trap fish.

7 (Focus Skill) How were the jobs of Powhatan men and women different?

_____

_____

Farming the Land

Powhatan women grew crops, such as corn, beans, and squash. They used hoes to break up the earth. Then, they used smaller sticks to dig holes where they put the seeds.

When European settlers came to North America, the Powhatan gave them food when the settlers had none. They taught the settlers how to hunt and grow crops, such as corn and tobacco, in Virginia.

Children in History

Pocahontas

Pocahontas was the daughter of the leader of the Powhatan. As a child, she played games with the children of Jamestown. Pocahontas married a settler named John Rolfe. They had a son. Her marriage helped bring about peace between American Indians and settlers for a time. Later, Pocahontas traveled with her family to England.

Powhatan Contributions

The Powhatan are known for making baskets, pottery, and carvings. We can see some of these artworks in American Indian communities and in museums.

American Indians believe in respect for nature. Long ago, they took from nature what they needed to live. They knew and cared for the land. They also used all parts of an animal so that nothing was wasted.

8 What do you think the children in the picture are learning to do?

_____

_____

63

1 SUMMARIZE Give one example of how the Powhatan used their environment.

_____

_____

_____

2 What were **dugout** canoes made from?

_____

Circle the letter of the correct answer.

3 What did the Powhatan do to help European settlers?

    A Made calendars based on the sun

    B Taught them to plant corn and tobacco

    C Built homes from mud bricks

    D Taught them to hunt buffalo

Activity

Make a chart. Use pictures and captions to show Powahatan homes, jobs, and ways of getting around.

The Lakota

Think about what it might be like if you often moved from one place to another.

Essential Questions

✔ How did the Lakota relate to their environment?
✔ How are American Indians of the past different from those of today?
✔ What are some contributions of American Indian culture to present-day life?

 HISTORY AND SOCIAL SCIENCE SOL
2.2, 2.4c, 2.4d

People of the Plains

![TextWork]

1 (Focus Skill) Underline the sentences that tell how the Lakota and the Powhatan were different.

For thousands of years, the Lakota have lived in what are today the states of North Dakota, South Dakota, Wyoming, and Montana. In the past, their ways of living were very different from those of the Powhatan. The land of the Plains was not good for farming. Instead, the Lakota hunted the buffalo that lived on the Plains.

Lakota Ways of Life

In hot weather, skins could be lifted to let the air in.

Lakota Homes

The Lakota lived in cone-shaped homes called **teepees**. To build a teepee, the Lakota set wooden poles in a circle and tied them at the top. Then they covered the poles with buffalo skins.

The teepees were easy to move when the Lakota went to a new place to hunt. During the winter, the buffalo skins kept Lakota families warm.

TextWork

❷ Underline the first step in making a teepee.

❸ Circle the sentence that tells how teepees were useful during winter.

Wood for teepee poles was hard to find on the Plains.

A travois

The Lakota made moccasins from buffalo skins.

Hunting and Gathering

Buffalo were very important to the Lakota. Groups of men hunted buffalo, using clubs and bows and arrows. Sometimes they chased the animals toward a cliff. The buffalo fell off and were killed.

The Lakota used almost every part of the buffalo. They ate its meat. They used the skins to make clothing. They made tools from the bones and horns. They even used the hooves to make glue.

The Lakota also hunted deer, elk, antelope, and birds. They ate fish that they caught and birds' eggs that they found.

The Lakota could not plant crops on the hard soil of the Plains. Lakota women gathered plants, such as onions, turnips, and potatoes. They also gathered strawberries, plums, and acorns.

5 Why did the Lakota not plant crops?

_____

_____

6 Write a title for the chart below.

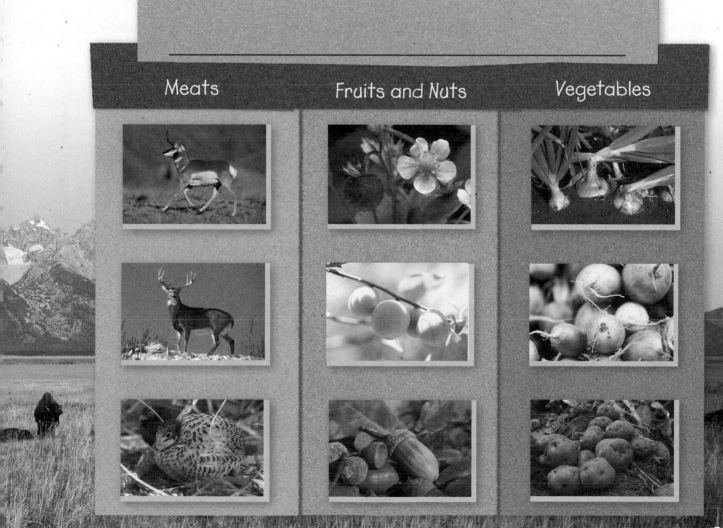

_____

| Meats | Fruits and Nuts | Vegetables |

Using Animals

The Lakota used dogs to help them carry things from place to place. They made a carrier called a **travois**, which was pulled by a dog.

Later, the Lakota learned to ride horses. They used the horses when hunting or traveling to trade with other American Indian groups. They also rode horses when they went to war.

TextWork

7 Which two animals did the Lakota use to help them?

_____

8 On the flowchart, circle the second step in making a travois.

Making a Travois

1 Tie two poles together at one end.

2 Tie a buffalo skin between the poles.

3 Attach travois to a dog.

4 Place things on the travois.

Lakota Contributions

Today, the Lakota carry on their culture in many ways. They have parties for special occasions. The hosts give gifts to all the guests. Long ago, these gifts included horses, blankets, and clothing. It is part of Lakota culture to be giving.

The Lakota remember their history and culture through stories. Some stories are about how things in nature came to be. Others tell about important people or events.

TextWork

9 Underline two ways the Lakota carry on their culture.

Lakota dancing at a powwow

71

1 **SUMMARIZE** Give one example of how the Lakota used their environment.

_____

_____

2 Explain why **teepees** were the best kind of homes for the Lakota.

_____

_____

Circle the letter of the correct answer.

3 Which of these foods did the Lakota eat?

A Corn

B Beavers

C Buffalo

D Squash

Writing

Imagine that you are going to a Lakota party long ago. Write about the gifts you might receive.

The Pueblo

Think about what it would be like to live in the desert.

Cliff Palace at Mesa Verde National Park

Essential Questions

✓ How did the Pueblo relate to their environment?
✓ How are American Indians of the past different from those of today?
✓ What are some contributions of American Indian culture to present-day life?

HISTORY AND SOCIAL SCIENCE SOL
2.2, 2.4c, 2.4d

TextWork

❶ What does the word <u>pueblo</u> mean?

_____

Life in the Desert

The land of the Southwest is very different from the Plains and the Eastern Woodlands. It has many mountains, cliffs, canyons, and mesas. A **mesa** is a flat-topped mountain with steep sides. The climate of the Southwest is very dry. Weeks can go by without rain.

Life has always been hard for the Pueblo who live in this area. The word <u>pueblo</u> comes from the Spanish word for <u>town</u>.

Pueblo Ways of Life EIP

Ladders were used to get inside.

74

Pueblo Homes

The Pueblo built their homes on the sides of cliffs or along canyon walls. Little rain fell in the desert, so few trees grew there.

Instead of wood, the Pueblo built homes from adobe. **Adobe** is sun-dried brick made of clay and straw. These homes, also called pueblos, sometimes had as many as five stories. The doors of the pueblos were on the roof.

TextWork

2 (Focus Skill) How were pueblos different from longhouses and teepees?

_____

_____

_____

Looms were used for weaving cloth.

Corn was ground up to make meal.

Clay ovens

75

Farming and Hunting

The Pueblo became good farmers over time. They grew corn, beans, squash, and melons. The Pueblo planted their crops below cliffs and in valleys. They dug ditches to carry water to the crops.

Corn was the Pueblo's most important food crop. Farmers used wooden tools to plant the seeds deep in the dry soil. They grew many colors of corn, including blue, red, yellow, and white.

Pueblo corn dance

76

Today, Pueblo people still grow corn near their towns. They have been farming corn for more than a thousand years. Women used to grind the corn between stones to make cornmeal. They used it to make tortillas, a kind of bread.

The Pueblo also used corn in soups and stews. Sometimes they added meat to the stews. They used to hunt deer, antelope, and rabbits. Today, they often use meat from sheep that they raise.

TextWork

❹ How did the Pueblo use corn in their cooking?

_____

_____

Pueblo women ground corn to make tortillas.

77

Trade Routes

The Pueblo grew cotton. They used it to make blankets and clothing. They traded these and other things for feathers, shells, buffalo hides, and dried meat.

The Pueblo did not always travel far to trade. They walked to nearby villages to trade with other American Indians. Those people then traded with still others farther away. In this way, items could travel long distances.

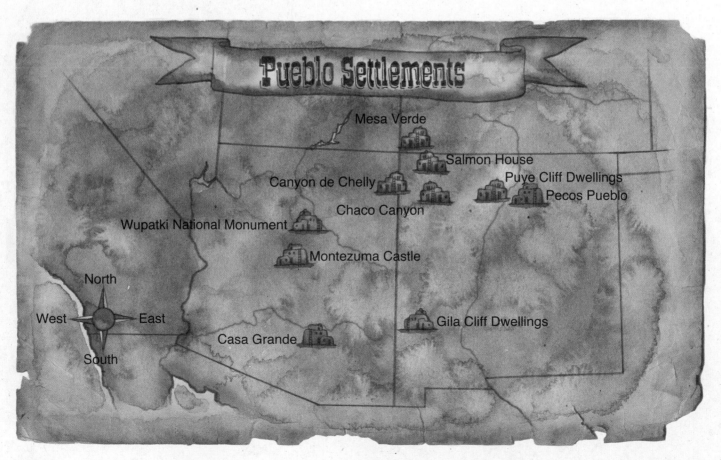

Pueblo Settlements

Mesa Verde
Salmon House
Canyon de Chelly
Puye Cliff Dwellings
Pecos Pueblo
Chaco Canyon
Wupatki National Monument
Montezuma Castle
North
West — East
South
Gila Cliff Dwellings
Casa Grande

Pueblo Contributions

Art is very important to the Pueblo. They make pots and baskets for decoration and storage. Parents pass on their skills to their children.

The Pueblo are also good weavers. Long ago, they wove yarn from cotton. Later, the Pueblo also began to use wool from sheep. They colored yarn using vegetable dyes. Every finished piece of cloth had a different design.

TextWork

6 Circle the kinds of art the Pueblo made.

7 What did the Pueblo use to color their weavings?

_____

8 What contributions have American Indians made that affect our lives today?

_____

_____

Similar but Different

The Powhatan, the Lakota, and the Pueblo people live in different regions of the United States. In the past, they had different kinds of homes, tools, and ways of living. But they all used their environment to meet their needs. Their cultures may have changed, but they still contribute to their communities in many ways.

Pueblo parents and grandparents teach children about Pueblo culture.

1 SUMMARIZE Give one example of how the Pueblo used their environment.

_____

_____

2 What is **adobe** made from?

_____

Circle the letter of the correct answer.

3 What does <u>pueblo</u> mean?

    A Town

    B Blanket

    C Desert

    D Corn

Writing

In books or on the Internet, look for pictures of the arts and crafts of the Pueblo people. Choose one, and write a description to present to the class.

Mix-Up

Mark an X on the picture that does not belong in each row.

1

2

3

82

Word Fun

Answer the questions.

Which letter do the words **longhouse**, **teepee**, and **pueblo** all have?

_____

What might food come in that is in the word **canoe**?

_____

What color is in the word **desert**?

_____

Answer the riddle.

What do both American Indians and baseball players have?

_____

Review and Test Prep

The Big Idea

American Indians have lived in Virginia and in other regions of North America for thousands of years.

Summarize the Unit

Focus Skill **Compare and Contrast** Fill in the chart to show how the Powhatan were like and different from the Lakota and the Pueblo.

Powhatan

lived in the Eastern Woodlands

_____

_____

_____

_____

Similar

used the resources around them to meet their needs

_____

_____

_____

_____

Lakota and Pueblo

lived on the Plains and in the desert Southwest

_____

_____

_____

_____

Use Vocabulary

Write the word under its meaning.

Word Bank

environment
p. 50

region
p. 52

climate
p. 52

dugout
p. 60

teepee
p. 67

adobe
p. 75

1 a boat made from a large, hollowed-out tree trunk

_____

2 sun-dried brick made from clay and straw

_____

3 an area of land with common features

_____

4 surroundings

_____

5 the kind of weather a place has over a long time

_____

85

Think About It

Circle the letter of the correct answer.

6 Which American Indian group hunted buffalo?

   A Pueblo

   B Powhatan

   C Lakota

   D Cherokee

7 The Powhatan placed a vent at the top of the longhouse to—

   F see who was coming

   G climb in through

   H help keep cool

   J let smoke out

8 What is the name of the region where the Pueblo lived?

   A Southwest

   B Northeast

   C Plains

   D Eastern Woodlands

⑨

Building a Teepee

Step 1

Step 2

Step 3

Step 4

Which step comes last?

  F Poles are set in a circle.

  G Poles are tied together at the top.

  H Buffalo skins are pinned to the ground.

  J Buffalo skins are pulled around poles.

Answer the question in a complete sentence.

⑩ What are some of the contributions of American Indian cultures to present-day life?

_____

_____

Look! It's the Time Museum. Let's go inside.

Eco is visiting the Time Museum, but there's a big problem. All the American Indian exhibits are mixed up! Can you help Eco? Play the game now, online or on CD.

Show What You Know

Writing Write a Travelogue
Imagine that you are an explorer meeting American Indians in North America. Write a description of a region you travel through and a group you meet.

Activity Role-Play
With a classmate, role-play how American Indians in one village might trade with those from another village, using items from the classroom.

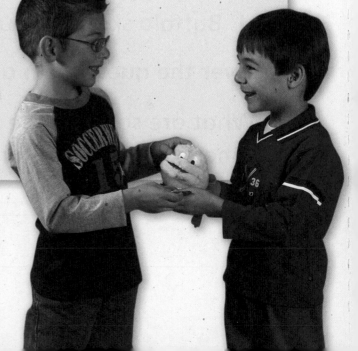

The World Around You

Assateague
Lighthouse,
Virginia

Spotlight on Standards

THE BIG IDEA The United States is a large country with many regions. The land and water in a region affect the ways people live, work, and play there.

HISTORY AND SOCIAL SCIENCE SOL
2.3, 2.4b, 2.4d, 2.5a, 2.5b, 2.6

89

Set the Stage

How does your environment affect the way you live?

"The way people live has changed over time."

Paddling down the
Dismal Swamp Canal

"It's fun to explore the many landforms of my state."

"A map can help me find my location."

91

Preview Vocabulary

community

My family has lived in our **community** for many years. (page 106)

population

Some towns have a small **population**.
(page 107)

transportation

Cars are one kind of **transportation** we use to get around. (page 108)

equator

Most countries near the **equator** have a very hot climate. (page 118)

map legend

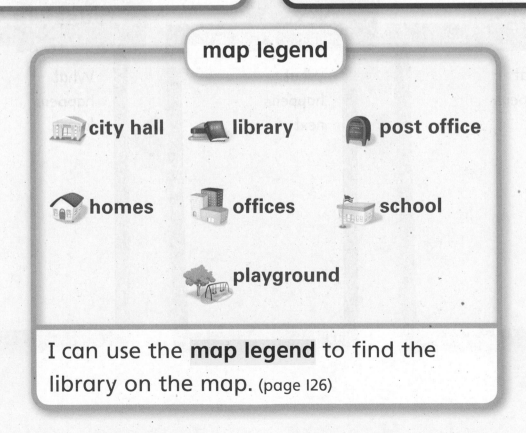

city hall   library   post office

homes   offices   school

playground

I can use the **map legend** to find the library on the map. (page 126)

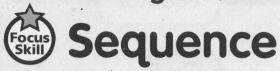

Sequence

Learn

■ Sequence is the order in which events happen. What happens first? What happens next? What happens last?

■ As you read, look for words such as <u>first</u>, <u>next</u>, <u>then</u>, <u>later</u>, <u>finally</u>, and <u>last</u>. These words give sequence clues.

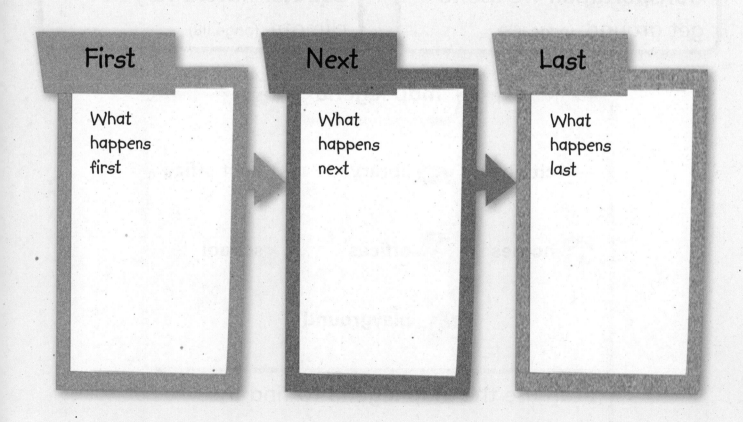

First — What happens first

Next — What happens next

Last — What happens last

Practice

Read the paragraph below. Underline the sentence that tells what happened after people began farming.

First, ancient people moved from place to place in search of food. Next, they learned how to grow crops and began farming. Last, they built villages and lived in one place for long periods of time.

Sequence

95

Apply

Read the following paragraph.

Farmers today have different jobs to do during each season of the year. First, they prepare the soil and plant the seeds in the spring. Next, they tend the crops during the summer. Farmers water the crops, weed the soil, and keep away pests. Last, they harvest the crops in the fall. During the winter, farmers rest and prepare for another year.

What can you add to the chart about the sequence of events in a farmer's year?

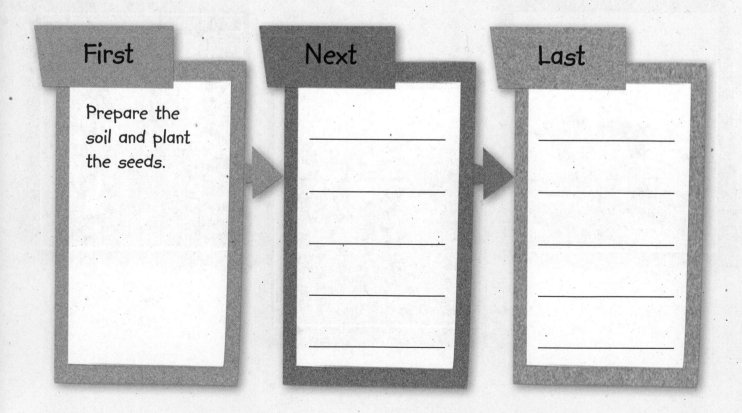

First

Prepare the soil and plant the seeds.

Next

_____

_____

_____

_____

Last

_____

_____

_____

_____

Understanding Your Environment

Think about how the place where you live is different from other places.

Meems Bottom Covered Bridge, Mount Jackson, Virginia

Essential Questions
✓ How is your environment different from other regions?
✓ How do people today relate to their environment?

 HISTORY AND SOCIAL SCIENCE SOL
2.3, 2.4b, 2.4d

❶ How are ancient people and people today alike?

_____

_____

Living in Your Environment

You have learned how the ancient Egyptians and the ancient Chinese used the land where they lived. You also read how American Indians used their environment to meet their needs. Today, people's lives are also affected by their environment.

Virginia Beach surfer

98

Land affects where people build their homes and even what they do for fun. People who live near the ocean may surf for fun. People who live in the mountains may hike, ski, or snowboard.

What people wear depends on the climate where they live. In hot climates, people wear loose clothing to stay cool. In places with cold winters, people wear heavy coats, hats, and scarves.

TextWork

2 What else might a person who lives near the ocean do for fun?

_____

_____

Virginia has many snowy days.

In the summer, people go hiking in the mountains.

3 (Focus Skill) What do farmers do after they clear the land?

_____

_____

Changing the Environment

Sometimes people must change the land where they live. Farmers clear their land by cutting down trees and moving rocks. Then they plow and plant seeds. Some farmers build fences so they can raise animals.

Builders may drain lakes to make more land to build on. By changing the environment, people are able to live in many different places.

A farm near Dayton, Virginia

People build roads, railroads, and bridges to help them get from place to place. They dig mines to get from the ground things such as coal, limestone, and diamonds.

In some areas, people dig wells to bring up water from the ground. In other places, they build dams across rivers. **Dams** are structures built to hold back water. Dams store water and keep rivers from flooding.

TextWork

❹ Circle the way people change their environment to help them get from place to place.

❺ What is a dam?

_____

_____

This dam in Virginia is used to make electricity.

Virginia has many coal mines.

6 Underline the two things geographers study.

Our Country's Geography

Geography is the study of Earth and the ways people use it. To make places on Earth easier to study, Earth is divided into regions. In each region, people use and change their environment in different ways.

The states in the middle of our country have good soil for growing crops. Many of our nation's farms and factories are located in this region.

Many states are located along the Atlantic Ocean. Fishing and shipbuilding are important jobs there.

States along the Pacific Ocean have forests and mountains. People visit the national parks in this region. Many people in these states work making movies, television shows, and music.

Lesson 1 Review

❶ SUMMARIZE How do people today change their environment?

_____

_____

❷ What is **geography**?

_____

Circle the letter of the correct answer.

❸ Which sentence BEST describes states along the Atlantic Ocean?

  A Most farms are located in this region.

  B Most factories are located in this region.

  C Fishing and shipbuilding are important jobs in this region.

  D People in this region work making movies.

Writing

Write a travel brochure about things that visitors can see and do in the region where you live.

104

Change Over Time

Think about how you have changed in the past year.

Essential Question
✓ How and why have communities changed over time?

SOL HISTORY AND SOCIAL SCIENCE SOL
2.3

❶ Underline examples of how changes can happen quickly.

Communities Change

Like people, communities change over time in some ways and stay the same in others. A **community** is a place where people live, work, and play together. Changes in a community usually happen slowly.

Some changes happen very fast. Disasters like earthquakes, hurricanes, and tornadoes can change the way a community looks in just a few hours.

Strong storms can knock down trees or cause flooding.

Getting Bigger

Communities grow as people move to them. The number of people living in a community is its **population**. As the population grows, new homes are built near the edges of communities.

A town's borders move outward to include these new areas. New roads are built. New businesses open. Some people move from cities to suburbs. Suburbs are smaller communities near a city.

TextWork

2 How does the population change as the community gets bigger?

_____

3 Underline changes that happen as a community grows.

Fairfax, Virginia, is a suburb near Washington D.C.

Changes in Transportation

Transportation is a way of moving people and things from one place to another. Long ago, most people used horses to pull wagons on dirt roads. Travel was very slow.

People wanted better and faster ways to travel. They built roads to connect new cities and towns. They also built canals to connect rivers.

In the past, people used ferry boats to cross Chesapeake Bay.

Later, people built railroads. Businesses could now get more things to markets faster. New businesses opened and new towns grew up along railroad tracks. People were able to travel farther by train than they had before.

Having cars let people live outside cities and drive to work. Then, airplanes made travel even easier. People are now able to travel across oceans in hours instead of weeks.

TextWork

5 (Focus Skill) Which came first, the railroad or the airplane?

_____

_____

Today, the Chesapeake Bay Bridge-Tunnel connects Virginia and Delaware.

6 Why were elevators needed in skyscrapers?

_____

_____

_____

New Inventions

Many new inventions have helped communities grow and change. People learned to use steel to build skyscrapers, or very tall buildings. Elevators were invented to carry people between floors.

Some inventions, like machines and computers, changed the ways people worked. People no longer had to make things by hand. They could work much faster than before.

Computers keep track of all the airplanes in the United States at the FAA command center in Herndon, Virginia.

Communication Changes

Communication is the sharing of ideas and information. Long ago, people wrote letters to friends and family who lived far away. Letters had to travel over land or by ship. That could take a long time.

Technology has created new ways of communication to connect people. Today, television, radio, phones, and the Internet let us know what is happening all over the world.

 **TextWork**

7 What is one tool that has made communication faster?

_____

_____

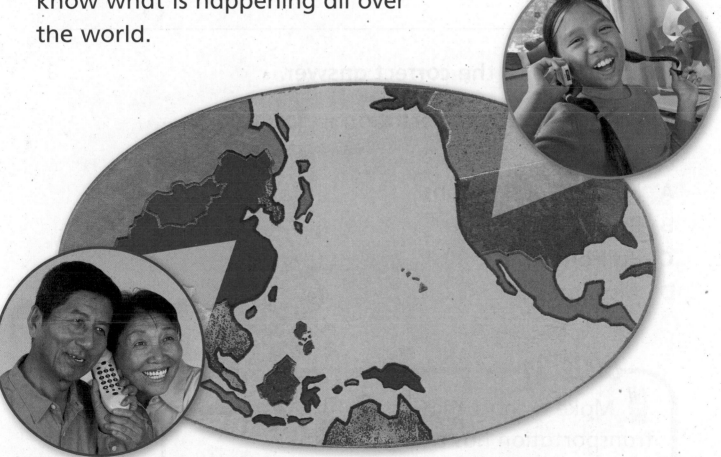

111

Lesson 2 Review

① **SUMMARIZE** How do communities change and grow?

_____

_____

② How might a community's **population** have changed when a railroad was built nearby?

_____

Circle the letter of the correct answer.

③ Which form of transportation is not used much today?

   A Horses and wagons

   B Boats

   C Railroads

   D Airplanes

Activity

Make a chart that shows how transportation has changed from long ago to today.

Communities Change and Grow

Think about a new building or neighborhood in your community.

Richmond, Virginia

Essential Question
✓ How and why has Richmond, Virginia, changed over time?

HISTORY AND SOCIAL SCIENCE SOL
2.3

❶ ⭐ Underline what Richmond was like in the past.

❷ In the pictures, circle some changes you see between Richmond long ago and today.

Richmond, Virginia

Long ago, Richmond looked different. It had dirt roads with no streetlights. Most buildings were made of brick. The city was much smaller than it is today.

Over time, more people have moved to Richmond. New houses and neighborhoods have been built. The roads have been paved. Downtown Richmond has many tall buildings.

Present

Past

There are many ways to learn about a community's past. You can visit museums and historic sites. You can look at old photographs or read books.

Some information is easier to understand in a graph. A **bar graph** uses bars to show the amounts or numbers of things. The graph below shows how the number of elementary schools in Richmond changed over time.

 **TextWork**

❸ On the bar graph, show how many schools Richmond has in 2010.

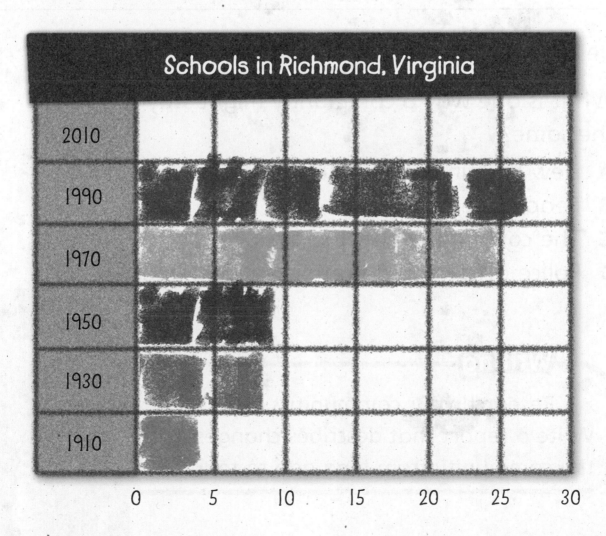

Schools in Richmond, Virginia

2010						
1990						
1970						
1950						
1930						
1910						

0   5   10   15   20   25   30

115

1 **SUMMARIZE** How and why has Richmond, Virginia, changed over time?

_____

_____

2 Describe what a **bar graph** shows.

_____

_____

Circle the letter of the correct answer.

3 What is one way a community might stay the same?

    A New buildings are built.

    B People use computers.

    C The community gets bigger.

    D Police officers and firefighters help people.

Writing

✏ Research your community's past. Write a report that describes changes in the community from long ago to today.

Mapping the World

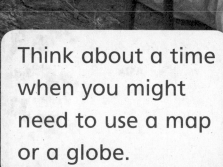

Think about a time when you might need to use a map or a globe.

Essential Questions

✓ Where are the seven continents, the five oceans, and the equator located on maps and globes?

✓ Where are the major rivers, lakes, and mountain ranges located on a map of the United States and the world?

HISTORY AND SOCIAL SCIENCE SOL
2.5a, 2.5b

117

Maps and Globes

✎ **TextWork**

❶ Underline the definition of equator.

❷ Circle the continent on which you live.

Maps and globes help people study Earth. They show location, or the place where something is. Maps and globes also show regions of the world and of our country.

The **equator** is an imaginary line that divides Earth into northern and southern halves. Most regions near the equator are very hot.

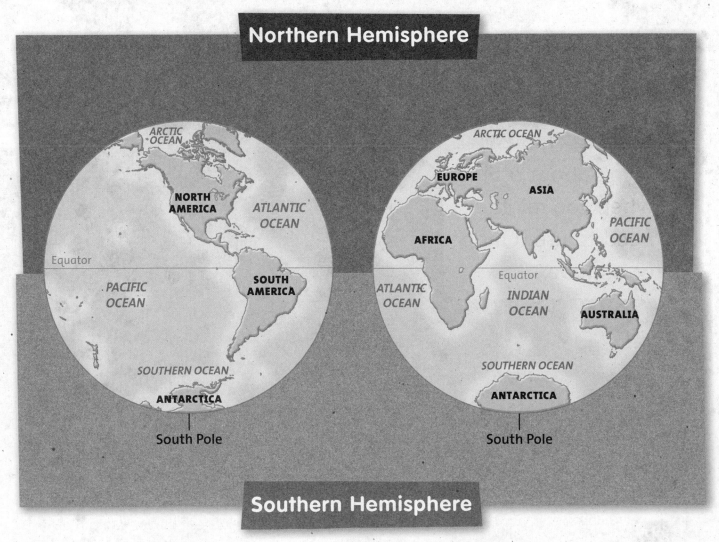

Northern Hemisphere

ARCTIC OCEAN

NORTH AMERICA

ATLANTIC OCEAN

Equator

PACIFIC OCEAN

SOUTH AMERICA

SOUTHERN OCEAN

ANTARCTICA

South Pole

ARCTIC OCEAN

EUROPE

ASIA

PACIFIC OCEAN

AFRICA

Equator

ATLANTIC OCEAN

INDIAN OCEAN

AUSTRALIA

SOUTHERN OCEAN

ANTARCTICA

South Pole

Southern Hemisphere

A **pole** is a point on Earth farthest from the equator. The farthest you can travel north from the equator is the North Pole. The farthest you can travel south is the South Pole. The regions close to each pole are very cold.

A **hemisphere** is half of Earth. The equator divides Earth into the Northern Hemisphere and the Southern Hemisphere.

TextWork

❸ Is North America in the Northern Hemisphere or the Southern Hemisphere?

_____

_____

Biography

Loyalty

Matthew F. Maury

Matthew F. Maury was born in Virginia. While in the United States Navy, he studied oceans and wind currents. He made maps that showed pathways for ships to travel. Maury also helped start the U.S. Naval Academy. His work made it possible for the first telegraph cable to be laid across the ocean floor.

119

Land and Water on Earth

Each of Earth's continents has different kinds of land. Australia has many deserts. In Europe, you can find tall, snowy mountains called the Alps.

Each continent also has different bodies of water. Some continents have long rivers. The Nile River, in Africa, is the longest river on Earth. The Huang He is an important river in Asia. Huang He means "Yellow River" in Chinese.

❹ Trace the Nile River on the map below.

❺ On which continent is the Great Victoria Desert located?

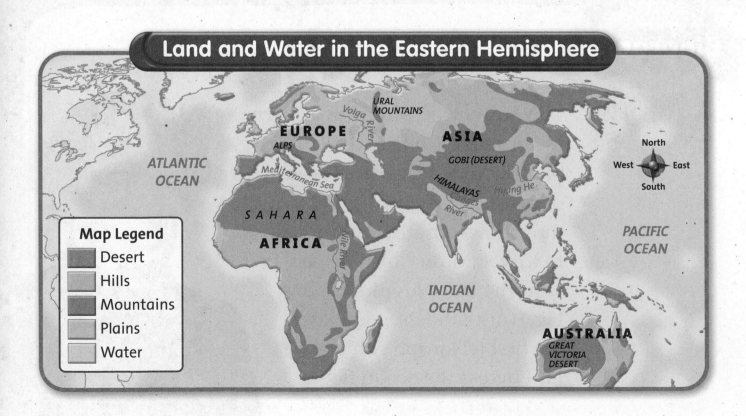

Land and Water in the Eastern Hemisphere

URAL MOUNTAINS
Volga River
EUROPE
ALPS
ATLANTIC OCEAN
Mediterranean Sea
ASIA
GOBI (DESERT)
HIMALAYAS
Ganges River
Huang He
North
West East
South
SAHARA
AFRICA
Nile River
PACIFIC OCEAN
INDIAN OCEAN
AUSTRALIA
GREAT VICTORIA DESERT

Map Legend
- Desert
- Hills
- Mountains
- Plains
- Water

120

Rivers in the United States

There are many rivers in the United States. Long ago, settlers to this country built towns along rivers. They used the rivers for food, water, and transportation.

The Mississippi River flows from Minnesota to the Gulf of Mexico. Many smaller rivers flow into the Mississippi River. The Rio Grande starts in Colorado. It makes up part of the border between the United States and Mexico.

TextWork

6 Which river starts in Colorado?

_____

Mississippi River

Lakes in the United States

The United States also has many lakes. The largest of these are the Great Lakes. They are located in the northern United States, along the border with Canada.

The largest of the Great Lakes is Lake Superior. Then come Lakes Huron, Michigan, and Erie. Lake Ontario is the smallest of the Great Lakes.

TextWork

7 (Focus Skill) Circle the name of the next largest of the Great Lakes after Lake Huron.

8 Which of the Great Lakes is located the farthest north?

Great Lakes

CANADA

North
West   East
South

Lake Superior

Lake Huron

Lake Michigan

Lake Ontario

Lake Erie

UNITED STATES

Lake Michigan

Mountains in the United States

Mountain ranges stretch across parts of the United States. A **mountain range** is a group of mountains. The Rocky Mountains are in the western United States. They stretch from British Columbia, in Canada, to New Mexico. Their highest peak is Mount Elbert. The Appalachian Mountains are in the eastern United States. They are covered with forests.

TextWork

9 Circle the name of the highest mountain in the Rockies.

10 Which mountain range is in the eastern United States?

_____

The Appalachian Mountains go through Virginia.

123

Lesson 4 Review

① **SUMMARIZE** Where can you locate the seven continents, the five oceans, and the equator?

_____

_____

_____

② What is a **hemisphere**?

_____

Circle the letter of the correct answer.

③ Which important river is located in Africa?

  A Huang He

  B Mississippi River

  C Rio Grande

  D Nile River

Activity

Draw a map of the United States. Label some of the rivers, lakes, and mountains you learned about.

Mapping Virginia

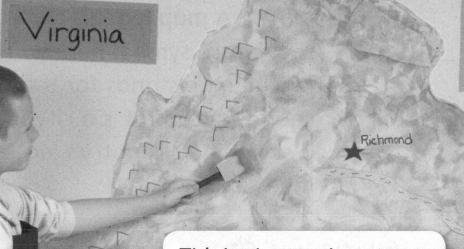

Think about where your community is located in Virginia.

Essential Questions

✓ Where is Virginia located on a map of the United States?
✓ What is included when making a map?

 HISTORY AND SOCIAL SCIENCE SOL
2.5b, 2.6

Making Maps

Look at the map. The **map title** helps you to know what the map shows.

Maps use symbols to show places. A **map legend** explains what each symbol means. The star on the map stands for the state capital. A **capital** is a city in which a state's or a country's leaders meet and work.

TextWork

1. (Focus Skill) What might you look at first when reading a map?

   _____

2. Circle the capital of Virginia on the map.

Richmond is the capital of Virginia.

A **compass rose** shows directions on a map. The four main directions are called cardinal directions. They are north, south, east, and west.

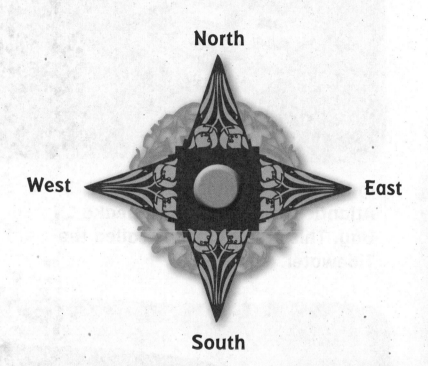

North

West

East

South

3 In which direction would you go to get from Richmond to Alexandria?

_____

4 From Danville, in which direction is Virginia's highest point?

_____

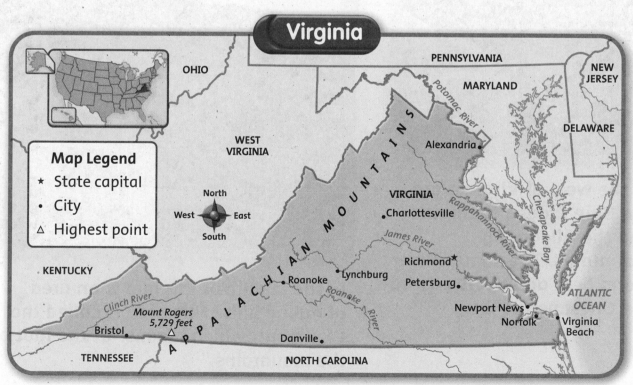

Virginia

Map Legend
★ State capital
• City
△ Highest point

OHIO

PENNSYLVANIA

MARYLAND

NEW JERSEY

DELAWARE

WEST VIRGINIA

Potomac River

Alexandria

North

West — East

South

VIRGINIA

Charlottesville

Rappahannock River

James River

Chesapeake Bay

KENTUCKY

APPALACHIAN MOUNTAINS

Richmond ★

Petersburg

Roanoke

Lynchburg

Clinch River

Roanoke River

Mount Rogers
5,729 feet
△

Bristol

Newport News

Norfolk

ATLANTIC OCEAN

Virginia Beach

Danville

TENNESSEE

NORTH CAROLINA

127

Virginia's Land and Water

![TextWork]

5 Circle the kinds of land in Virginia.

6 Underline the kinds of water in Virginia.

In the east, Virginia borders the Atlantic Ocean and Chesapeake Bay. This area of land is called the Tidewater.

In the west of Virginia are the Blue Ridge Mountains and the Allegheny Mountains. The James River starts here and flows east to the Chesapeake Bay.

In the middle of Virginia is an area of rolling hills. This area is called the Piedmont, which means "at the foot of the mountains."

Lesson 5 Review

1 SUMMARIZE Where is Virginia located on a map of the United States?

_____

_____

2 What does a **compass rose** show?

_____

Circle the letter of the correct answer.

3 Which of Virginia's regions has rolling hills?

   A Tidewater

   B Eastern part

   C Western part

   D Piedmont

Activity

Make a map of a familiar place, such as your bedroom or a classroom. Write a map title. Use symbols and a map legend to show places.

129

What Doesn't Belong?

**Look at this picture of life long ago.
Circle four things that do not belong.**

Missing Letters

Each word is missing the same letter. When you find it, use the letter to answer the riddle.

Word	Clue
d ? m	a huge structure built to hold back water
c h ? n g e	what happens when something becomes different
p o p u l ? t i o n	the number of people living in a community
e q u ? t o r	an imaginary line that divides Earth

What islands are good to eat?

T h e   S ? n d w i c h   I s l ? n d s

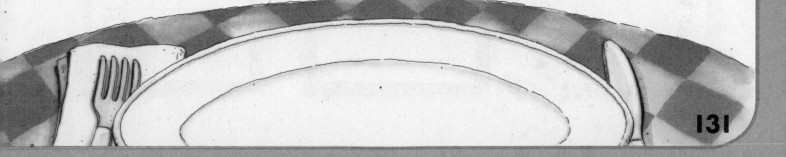

131

Review and Test Prep

The Big Idea

The United States is a large country with many regions. The land and water in a region affect the ways people live, work, and play there.

Summarize the Unit

Focus Skill **Sequence** Fill in the chart to show changes in transportation.

First

People used horses to pull wagons on dirt roads.

Next

_____

_____

_____

_____

_____

_____

_____

Last

_____

_____

_____

_____

_____

_____

_____

Use Vocabulary

Complete each sentence.

① People use a form of _____

to get from one place to another.

② A country with a large

_____ has many citizens.

③ To understand what each symbol on a

map means, use a _____.

④ The _____ is an imaginary

line that divides Earth into the

Northern Hemisphere and the Southern

Hemisphere.

⑤ Your neighborhood and your school are

part of your _____.

> **Word Bank**
>
> **community**
> p. 106
>
> **population**
> p. 107
>
> **transportation**
> p. 108
>
> **bar graph**
> p. 115
>
> **equator**
> p. 118
>
> **map legend**
> p. 126

Think About It

Circle the letter of the correct answer.

6 What might people who live in hot climates do?

A Use animal furs to make clothing

B Go snowboarding

C Wear loose clothing to stay cool

D Burn wood for heat

7 Which shows how a new invention might change a community?

F More people are born.

G Skyscrapers are built.

H A hurricane knocks down houses.

J The climate becomes warmer.

8 The Rio Grande is located on the continent of—

A Asia

B Africa

C South America

D North America

9

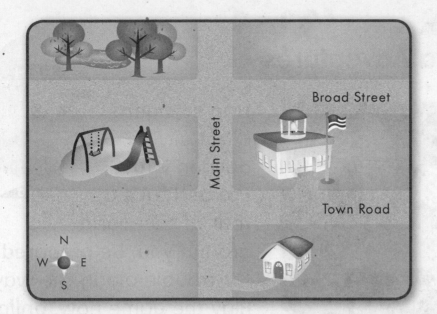

In which direction would someone walk to get from the playground to the school?

F East

G West

H North

J South

Answer each question in a complete sentence.

10 What do you think will happen to a community if people move away?

_____

_____

11 How did the first people who made maps and globes learn about the world?

_____

_____

We'll be able to see the world from this hot air balloon.

Hop on board a hot air balloon with Eco and take a tour of the world around you. Be prepared for trouble along the way. Play the game now, online or on CD.

Show What You Know

Writing **Write an Advertisement**
Write an advertisement for your city, giving reasons why people might want to move there. List details that explain what makes your community a good place to live.

Activity **Draw a Map**
Draw a map of Virginia. Show the state's land and water and the ways people use them.

The Marketplace

Meadows of Dan,
Virginia

Spotlight
on Standards

THE BIG IDEA People use resources to meet
their needs.

 HISTORY AND SOCIAL SCIENCE SOL
2.7, 2.8, 2.9

137

Set the Stage

How do people earn, spend, and save money?

"I earned money to buy a gift for my brother."

"I think about the cost before I choose what I will buy."

"I use money I saved to buy what I want."

Preview Vocabulary

barter

People can **barter** instead of using money.
(page 158)

money

My family spends **money** for food and clothing. (page 159)

producer

This **producer** makes and sells baked goods. (page 164)

consumer

You are a **consumer** when you buy goods. (page 165)

scarcity

Because of **scarcity**, people make choices about what to make or buy. (page 166)

Categorize and Classify

Learn

■ When you categorize and classify, you sort things into groups.

■ Decide what each group will be called.

■ Place each thing in a group.

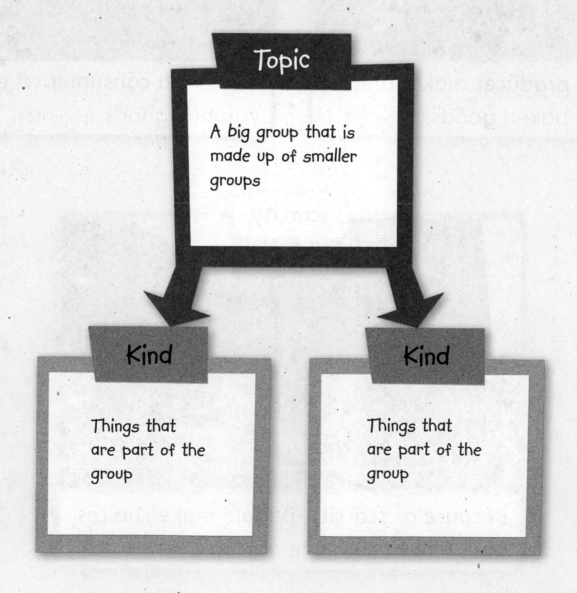

Topic

A big group that is made up of smaller groups

Kind

Things that are part of the group

Kind

Things that are part of the group

Practice

Underline the category of exercise. Then circle the things classified as exercise.

There are many things you can do for fun. You might play sports such as basketball and soccer. You might play with toys, such as dolls or small race cars. You might exercise by going for a walk or jumping rope.

Categorize

Classify

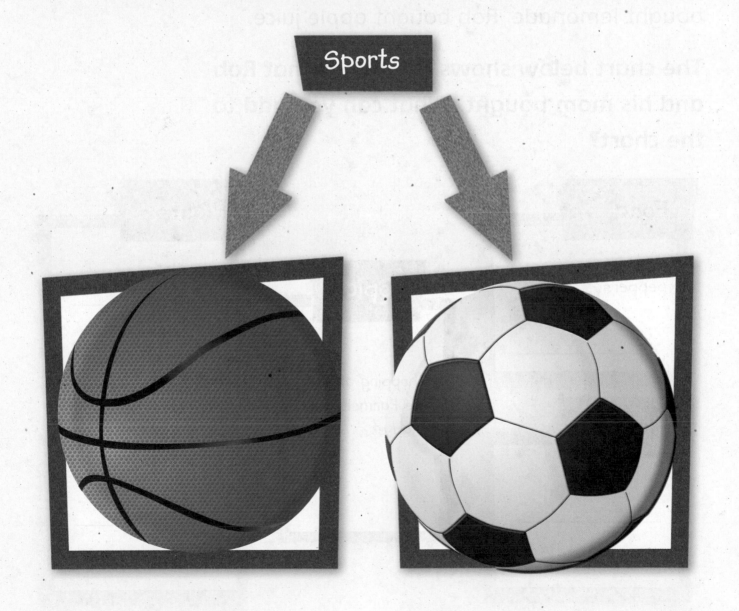

Sports

Apply

Read the following paragraph.

Rob and his mom shopped at the Farmers Market. They bought food, plants, clothes, and drinks. They bought peppers and cucumbers. Mom chose roses and daisies for the garden. Rob bought a T-shirt and a hat. When they finished shopping, they bought drinks. Mom bought lemonade. Rob bought apple juice.

The chart below shows the things that Rob and his mom bought. What can you add to the chart?

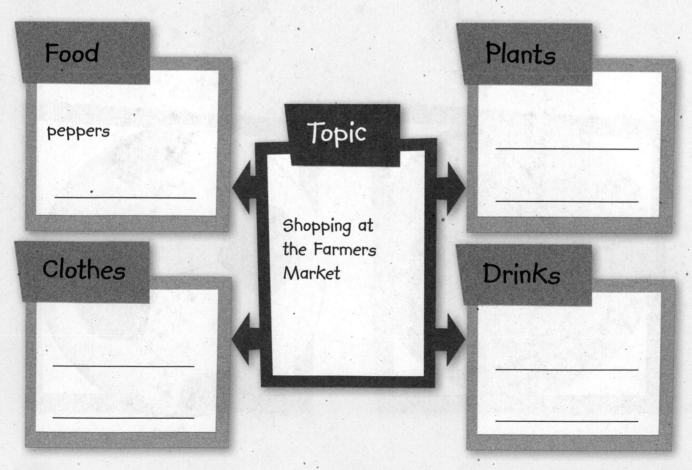

Using Resources

Think about what some of the things you use every day are made from.

Essential Question

✔ What are natural, human, and capital resources?

HISTORY AND SOCIAL SCIENCE SOL
2.7

Natural Resources

A **natural resource** is something found in nature that people can use. People use natural resources to live. For example, people use water for drinking, cooking, cleaning, and growing plants.

People also use water to make electricity. They build dams on rivers. Water flows through the inside of the dam and turns big machines that make electricity.

TextWork

❶ (Focus Skill) Underline some examples of natural resources.

❷ What can be used to make electricity?

146

People use soil to grow all kinds of plants. They grow wheat to make bread. They grow cotton to make clothing.

Some farmers grow trees that make fruits and nuts. People also use wood from trees to make furniture and to build homes.

People can find coal, oil, and natural gas underground. They can make these resources into fuels. A **fuel** is something that can be burned for heat or energy.

TextWork

❸ Underline some uses for trees.

❹ Look at the table. Which natural resource can be used to make plastic toys?

_____

How People Use Resources

Natural Resources	Ways People Use Natural Resources			
Trees	fruits/nuts	furniture	lumber	paper
Iron	steel beams	paper clips	bicycle	tools
Oil	plastic toys	medicines	candles	fuel

5 (Focus Skill) Circle the human resource in the picture.

6 Underline the sentence that tells what a factory is.

Human Resources

Virginians work at many different jobs. Virginia farmers grow many kinds of crops, including potatoes, soybeans, peanuts, and apples. Miners find coal and limestone underground. Some people work in factories. A **factory** is a building in which people use machines to make things. All of these workers are **human resources**.

Capital Resources

All the tools and buildings used to make a product are called **capital resources**. These include factory buildings and the machines inside them. They also include the trucks that move finished products from one place to another. Hammers, lawn mowers, and computers are all examples of capital resources.

TextWork

7 What are capital resources?

_____

_____

8 Name one capital resource a painter might use.

_____

149

9 Underline one way we can save our resources.

Caring for Our Resources

Every year, the number of people living on Earth gets larger. With so many people using Earth's resources, we must find ways to protect our resources and make them last longer.

One way to save resources is by recycling. When we **recycle**, we use the materials in old things to make new things. We can recycle paper, cans, and glass.

Wind turbines

Another way to save resources is to use old resources in new ways. Today, scientists are finding new ways to make energy and fuels.

We can now heat and cool our homes using energy from the sun or from wind. We can run our cars on electricity or fuels made from different plants. Some cars run on the oil used to make French fries!

TextWork

10 Circle the natural resources that are being used in new ways.

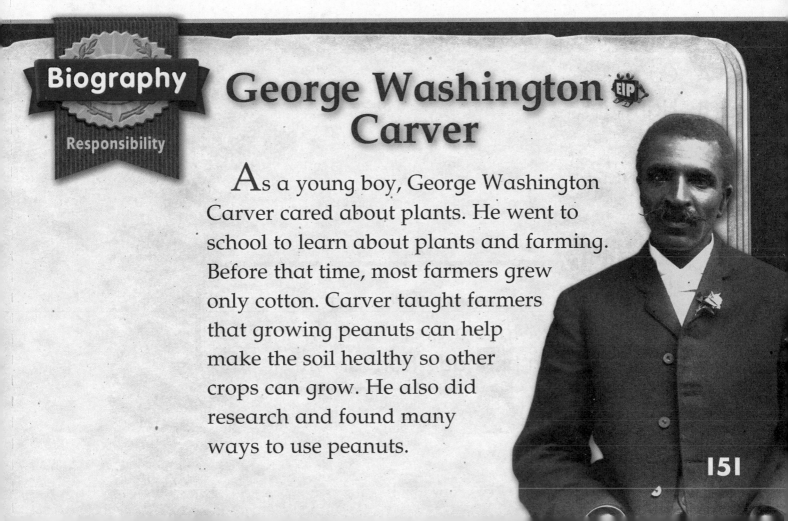

Biography

Responsibility

George Washington Carver

As a young boy, George Washington Carver cared about plants. He went to school to learn about plants and farming. Before that time, most farmers grew only cotton. Carver taught farmers that growing peanuts can help make the soil healthy so other crops can grow. He also did research and found many ways to use peanuts.

❶ **SUMMARIZE** What are natural, human, and capital resources?

_____

_____

❷ What do workers in a **factory** do?

_____

_____

Circle the letter of the correct answer.

❸ Which is a capital resource?

    A Coal

    B Hammer

    C Tree

    D Farmer

Activity

Choose a natural resource that comes from Virginia. Make a chart to show the things that can be made from or with it.

Goods and Services

Think about the kinds of things you and your family buy every week.

Cary Street, Richmond, Virginia

Essential Question

✓ How do people rely on goods and services?

SOL HISTORY AND SOCIAL SCIENCE SOL
2.8

153

Goods

Workers in a community make goods. **Goods** are things that can be bought and sold. Some goods, such as cars, are made. Others, such as vegetables, are grown.

Some communities are known for the goods that are made or grown there. The cities of Norfolk, Newport News, and Portsmouth are known for shipbuilding. Companies in these cities build aircraft carriers and submarines.

TextWork

❶ What are things that can be bought and sold?

_____

❷ In the picture, circle the goods that are important to Virginia.

Some people in Norfolk work building ships. Others load them with goods to be shipped to other cities.

154

Services

Many workers in a community provide, or offer, services. A **service** is work done for others for pay. Services can be things such as haircuts and music lessons.

Tourism is an important service in Virginia. Tourism is the selling of goods and services to people who visit a place for fun. People visit Virginia's museums, national parks, and monuments.

Tourism workers in Williamsburg teach visitors about the city's historic sites.

155

1 SUMMARIZE How do people rely on goods and services?

_____

_____

2 Name some examples of **goods** that are grown.

_____

_____

Circle the letter of the correct answer.

3 Which is a service that tourism workers might provide?

 A Selling tickets

 B Baking bread

 C Cutting hair

 D Fishing

Writing

Write a paragraph that tells about a time when you used a service in your community.

Buying and Selling

Think of a time when you traded something with a friend.

Essential Question

✓ What is the difference between using barter and using money in exchange for goods and services?

 HISTORY AND SOCIAL SCIENCE SOL
2.8

157

Barter

TextWork

① 🌟 What was used to trade long ago?

_____

② Find the picture of wampum. What do you think it is made of?

_____

Did you know that long ago people traded salt, shells, beads, or feathers to get goods and services? People traded with one another to get what they could not make or grow themselves. For example, a farmer could trade grain to a fisher for fish. This kind of trade is called **barter**.

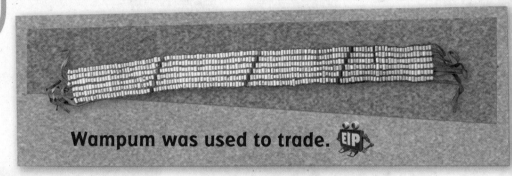

Wampum was used to trade.

American Indians traded animal furs for tools and cloth.

Money

Today we use coins, paper bills, and checks to buy what we want. We call this **money**.

Money was first made because it was easier to carry and count than goods used to trade were. People used coins made from silver or gold to buy goods and services. However, a bag of coins could be heavy, too. Then, about one thousand years ago, the Chinese began making paper money.

TextWork

3 Why was paper money invented?

_____

_____

_____

early American greenback

ancient coins

Chinese money

159

❹ Underline the sentence that tells what the word <u>business</u> means.

❺ Why do people work?

_____

_____

Earning Money

People must work to earn money. Think of all the jobs people do in the world. Most people work in some kind of business. In a **business**, workers make or sell goods or services.

Earning and Spending

160

Whatever jobs people do, they depend on one another. The money one person earns at a job will be paid to someone else for a good or service.

6 Look at the chart. How do people depend on one another?

_____

_____

_____

1 **SUMMARIZE** How is using money different from barter?

_____

_____

_____

2 Name a **business** in your community.

_____

Circle the letter of the correct answer.

3 What do most people use to buy goods and services today?

  A Wampum

  B Gold

  C Money

  D Food

Writing

Explain why jobs are important to you and your family.

Making Wise Choices

Think about some choices you made today and how you made them.

Producers

You know now that you depend on the people who make goods and give services. These people are called **producers**. Producers make or grow the food we need. They put together the cars we drive. They make the movies we watch. Producers also sell all the products made by other producers.

TextWork

❶ Circle the three products that are made by producers.

❷ (Focus Skill) Name other producers in your community.

_____

_____

Craftworkers are producers. This artist makes beautiful birdhouses to sell.

Consumers

We are all consumers. A **consumer** is a person who buys and uses goods and services. Consumers depend on producers to provide the things they need and want. Producers depend on consumers to buy their goods and services. Anywhere people buy and sell goods is called a market.

TextWork

3 Underline the sentence that tells why producers depend on consumers.

Children in History

Alexandra "Alex" Scott

When Alex Scott was a baby, she became sick with cancer. When she was four years old, she wanted to raise money to help find a cure for children's cancer. Alex set up a lemonade stand. Soon there were lemonade stands all over the country. They were raising money for hospitals to help sick children.

So Many Choices

People have to make choices about what they buy. First, most people buy things they need to live, such as food, clothing, and a home. Then they buy things they want, such as toys or jewelry.

Sometimes there is scarcity of a kind of product that people want to buy. When there is **scarcity**, there is not enough of something. People may have to spend more money for scarce products.

TextWork

4 Circle the things people need to buy.

5 What does <u>scarcity</u> mean?

_____

_____

Clare must choose how best to spend her money.

166

Clare is going shopping, but she does not have enough money to buy everything she wants. Money can be scarce, too. Clare must decide what to give up to get what she wants most.

Clare loves to play video games. She also wants a fun-looking watch she saw. Clare even wants to learn how to ride horses. What will she be willing to give up so she gets what she wants?

 **TextWork**

6 Circle the product you think Clare might choose to buy. Tell why.

_____

_____

Spend or Save

People know that they cannot have everything they want. Families must plan how to spend and save their money. They might want to save money for a new car, a new home, or a vacation.

Having a budget can help you and your family spend money wisely. A **budget** is a plan for spending money. A budget should show what is most important and least important to the family.

Familes save money so that children can go to college.

168

1 SUMMARIZE How do producers and consumers depend on one another?

_____

_____

2 How can **scarcity** affect the price of something?

_____

Circle the letter of the correct answer.

3 What can help a family spend money wisely?

   A Bank

   B Scarcity

   C Budget

   D Market

Activity

Draw pictures of six things that you would like to have. Arrange them in order from what you want most to what you want least.

ICE CREAM

CONES

T-SHIRT SALE

SANDWICH

FRESH PRODUCE

LEMON

Face
Painting

PIZZA

Marketplace

Look at the picture.

Which of these people sells strawberries?

Who is offering a service?

Find and circle a consumer. Tell what he or she is doing.

_____

_____

_____

Review and Test Prep

The Big Idea

People use resources to meet their needs.

Summarize the Unit

Focus Skill **Categorize and Classify** Fill in the chart to show the parts of a market.

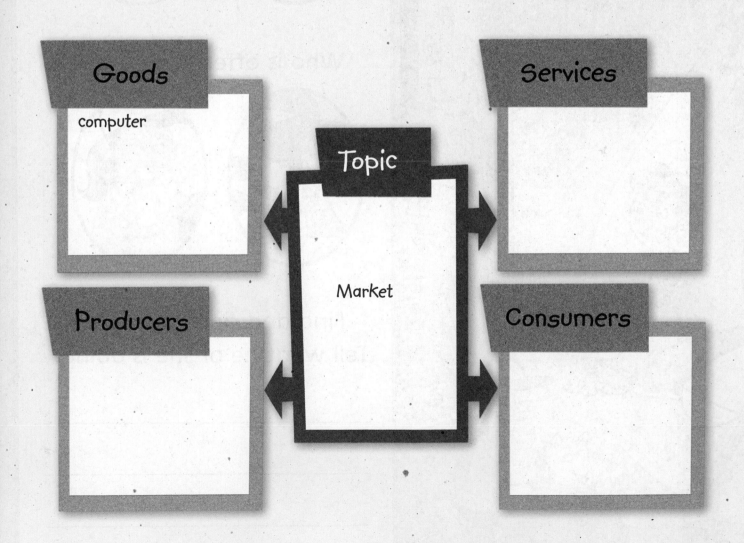

Goods

computer

Services

Topic

Market

Producers

Consumers

Use Vocabulary

Write the word under its meaning.

Word Bank

capital
resources
p. 149

barter
p. 158

money
p. 159

producer
p. 164

consumer
p. 165

scarcity
p. 166

❶ coins, paper bills, and checks used in exchange for goods and services

_____

❷ a person who uses resources to make goods or provide services

_____

❸ not being able to meet all wants at the same time

_____

❹ the trading of goods and services without the use of money

_____

❺ a person who uses goods and services

_____

Think About It

Circle the letter of the correct answer.

6 Which of these is a natural resource?

A Plastic

B Workers

C Water

D Tractors

7 What kind of resources are tools and machines?

F Natural resources

G Human resources

H Capital resources

J Money resources

8 Most people work to—

A keep busy

B earn money

C learn new things

D help others

9

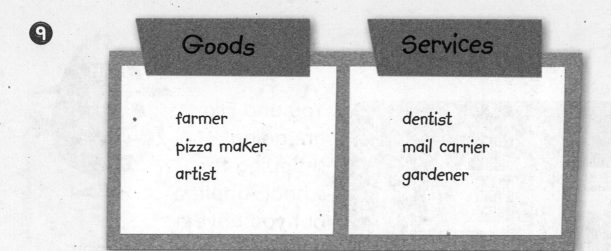

Goods	Services
farmer	dentist
pizza maker	mail carrier
artist	gardener

Which of these people provides a service?

F Mail carrier

G Artist

H Farmer

J Pizza maker

Answer each question in a complete sentence.

10 Why might a good or a service become scarce?

_____

_____

11 How do people make choices about what to buy?

_____

_____

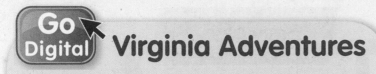

Help me do my back-to-school shopping.

You and Eco are going shopping for school supplies, but you have a limited amount of money. Can you afford everything Eco needs? Play the game now, online or on CD.

ECO

Show What You Know

Writing Write a Report
How would your life be different if you had to make all the goods you wanted?

Activity Design an Ad
Think of something to sell. Why might people want to buy it? Draw an ad to sell your item. Use details to describe the item.

Good Citizens

Spotlight on Standards

THE BIG IDEA People in communities must follow rules and respect one another's rights.

SOL **HISTORY AND SOCIAL SCIENCE SOL**
2.10a, 2.10b, 2.10c, 2.10d, 2.10e, 2.12a, 2.12b

Set the Stage

How do you show that you are a good citizen?

Ballot
Mrs. Rodriguez's Class

Class Leader
Líder de la clase

Nicholas
Teresa
Avery

"Voting is an important part of being a citizen in our country."

Virginia State Capitol
Building in Richmond

"Good citizens follow
rules and laws."

"Good citizens like to
help other people."

Preview Vocabulary

citizen

Citizens can make their community a good place to live by helping each other. (page 186)

law

Laws help keep people safe. (page 187)

responsibility

It is my **responsibility** to help my family. (page 186)

vote

People **vote** to choose their leaders. (page 194)

diversity

You can see **diversity** in a community's culture. (page 202)

Focus Skill

Generalize

Learn

■ To generalize is to make a statement about a group of facts.

■ To make a generalization, think about how the facts are related.

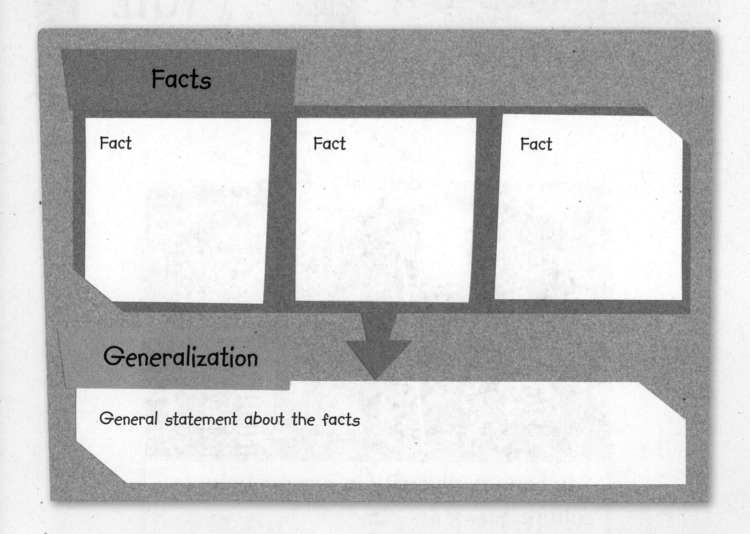

Facts

| Fact | Fact | Fact |

Generalization

General statement about the facts

Practice

Underline the generalization in the paragraph below.

A community's resources belong to everyone. Community members share water and electricity. They use public parks and playgrounds. They work together to make their community a good place to live. Good citizens must take care of the resources they share.

Fact

Apply

Read the following paragraph.

There are many ways that people can save, or conserve, resources. You can conserve water by turning off the tap when you brush your teeth. You can conserve trees by using less paper. You can also plant trees to take the place of trees that have been cut down. You can conserve gasoline by using cars less often. Instead, you can walk or ride your bike.

What facts can you add to the chart below?

Facts

You can conserve water by turning off the tap when you brush your teeth.

_____

_____

_____

_____

Generalization

Conservation is the act of saving resources to make them last longer.

Being a Good Citizen

Think about the chores you have at home and at school.

Essential Question
✔ What are some responsibilities of a good citizen?

 HISTORY AND SOCIAL SCIENCE SOL
2.10a, 2.10c, 2.10d, 2.10e

① Underline something that each citizen has.

Citizens Have Responsibilities

You and your family are citizens of your community. A **citizen** is a person who lives in and belongs to a community. Each citizen has different responsibilities. A **responsibility** is something you should take care of or do.

Bike Safety

1. Wear a helmet.
2. Follow traffic laws.
3. Stay on bike path.

Citizens must help take care of their schools and communities. Everyone can set a good example by following rules and laws. A **law** is a rule that all citizens must follow. Wearing your seat belt is a law that keeps you safe.

You share the place where you live with other members of the community. You can help keep the community clean. You can also work as a volunteer to help others.

TextWork

2 What is another word for law?

_____

Biography

Citizenship

Robin Dunbar

Each day at work, Robin Dunbar acts like a princess. She dresses like Princess Elizabeth, for whom the Elizabeth River is named. She teaches people that it is important to take care of the river. She visits schoolchildren to explain that part of being a good citizen means taking care of nature and keeping our communities clean.

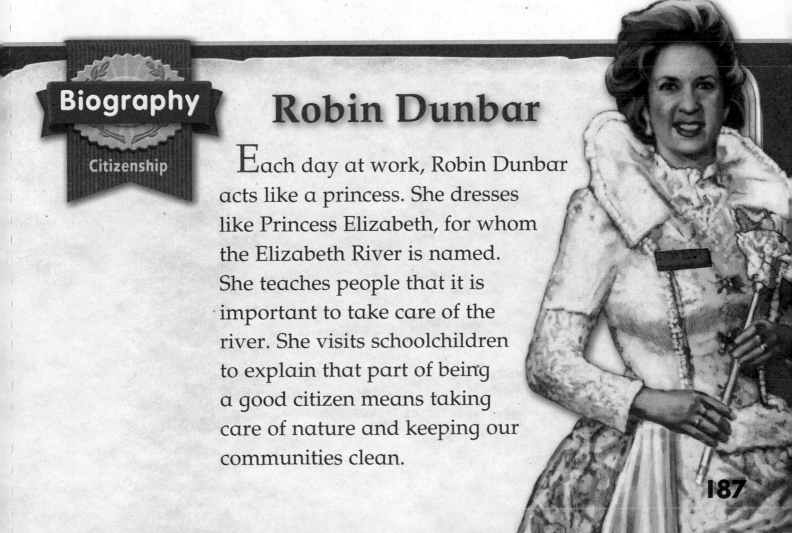

187

Respecting the Rights and Property of Others

All citizens have a responsibility to respect the rights of other people. A **right** is something people are free to do. People have the right to be safe, to have their own opinions, and to live where they choose. You should always respect others by treating them as you want to be treated.

❸ What is a <u>right</u>?

_____

_____

❹ Underline some examples of rights people have.

Respect others' property

Listen to others

188

Being careful with someone's property is another way to show respect. Property is a thing or place that belongs to a person. If you borrow school supplies, a book, or a game, you should return it the way it was when you got it.

Some property, such as parks and schools, belongs to the public. A good citizen respects public property and does nothing to damage it.

 **TextWork**

5 Circle the picture that shows someone respecting others' property.

6 (Focus Skill) Underline the sentence that tells what public property is.

Stay on path!

7 What is another example of self-discipline?

_____

_____

_____

Children Have Responsibilities

You have a responsibility to do what is right and fair. To do this, you must have self-discipline. That means that you should think about your choices in a calm and careful way. You should control your temper when you are upset.

You must also have self-reliance. That means that you should do things for yourself. You should not ask others to do your work for you.

You must also practice honesty and trustworthiness. Honesty is telling the truth and making sure your friends know how you feel about things. Trustworthiness is keeping promises and finishing work that is given to you.

People grow through experience if they meet life honestly and courageously. This is how character is built.

— Eleanor Roosevelt

Lesson 1 Review

1 **SUMMARIZE** What are some responsibilities of a good citizen?

_____

_____

2 What is one **law** citizens in a community must follow?

_____

_____

Circle the letter of the correct answer.

3 People show respect for others when they—

   A damage public property

   B forget to return a book

   C ignore others' opinions

   D treat others as they want to be treated

Bike Safety
1. Wear a helmet.
2. Follow traffic laws.
3. Stay on bike path.

Activity

Make a poster that shows you being a good citizen in your school and community.

Virginia's Government

Think about a time when you had to choose a leader.

Essential Question

✔ How are state and local government officials elected?

 HISTORY AND SOCIAL SCIENCE SOL
2.10b, 2.12a

Making Decisions

TextWork

❶ What is a decision you had to make today?

_____

_____

❷ Underline the sentence that tells what a vote is.

You make decisions every day. At home, you may choose what to wear and what to eat. In school, you choose how to do your work.

When groups make decisions, they must talk about what to do. People often have different opinions. Groups may vote to make choices or decide what to do about a problem. A **vote** is a choice that gets counted. The choice that gets the most votes wins.

This girl is deciding which book to read.

194

In school, your class may vote on what game to play or what animal to have for a class pet. You might also vote to choose a class leader.

Communities and our country work the same way. Adult citizens vote to choose people to lead us. They also vote for or against new laws. Voting is an important responsibility.

 **TextWork**

❸ Underline the two things adult citizens might vote for.

❹ Circle the picture that shows a ballot.

Ballot for Class Leader

☑ Haley

☐ Sam

☐ Ashley

☐ Mel

5 (Focus Skill) Why do you think a community needs a government?

_____

_____

6 Underline what happens at an election.

Community Government

All communities have a **government**, or a group of citizens who run the community. The government makes laws to keep citizens safe. It also helps make sure citizens get along.

Citizens choose many of their government leaders at events called **elections**. People choose the leaders who they think will do the best job.

Citizens voting in Clifton, Virginia

name Gavin

Elected Officials   2.12.a

Read pages 197-199 in your textbook. Answer the
questions below.

Each city or town in Virginia has a
Govrmit.

What does a mayor do? ron the
site

What does the Virginia Constitution explain? _____

_____

_____

_____

What is the job of a governor? _____

_____

_____

Each city or town in Virginia has a government. Most cities are run by a **mayor**. The city council helps the mayor run the city government. A council is a group of people who make laws.

The mayor makes sure the laws are followed and suggests new laws. In some cities, the council chooses a city manager to help run the government.

 TextWork

7 What does a mayor do?

_____

_____

8 Circle the picture that shows where a city council works.

Mayor Susan P. Irving of Waverly, Virginia

The mayor and city council work in City Hall.

197

State Government

The Virginia Constitution is a written set of rules that the state government and citizens must follow. It explains how the government is set up. It also lists the rights of Virginia's citizens.

The state government makes laws for all Virginians. A **governor** is the leader of the state's government. The governor makes sure the state's laws are obeyed.

Governor Tim Kaine EIP

The governor works with the General Assembly to make new laws. The members of the General Assembly suggest laws. Then the governor decides whether to sign the laws. The state's courts decide if the laws are fair and if they follow the Virginia Constitution.

TextWork

❶ What does the General Assembly do?

_____

_____

Leaders

	Principal
	Mayor
	Governor
	President

Virginia General Assembly

Lesson 2 Review

❶ SUMMARIZE How are state and local government officials elected?

_____

_____

❷ What is the job of a **governor**?

_____

Circle the letter of the correct answer.

❸ The Virginia Constitution—

   A makes new laws

   B tells how to choose a mayor

   C tells the rules the state government must follow

   D gives the rules for choosing a class leader

Writing

Imagine that you are running for mayor of your town. Write a speech that tells how you will make the community a better place in which to live.

The Citizens of Virginia

> Think about a holiday we all celebrate together.

Essential Questions

✓ How do people of diverse ethnic origins, customs, and traditions participate in and contribute to their communities in the United States?

✓ How are people of different ethnic origins and customs united as Americans?

HISTORY AND SOCIAL SCIENCE SOL
2.12b

How We Are Different

In some ways, you are like your neighbors and other people around the world. In some ways, you are different. People have come from many countries to live in Virginia. They have brought **diversity**, or different ideas and ways of living. You can find diversity in people's food, clothing, music, languages, and beliefs.

Virginians enjoy listening to different kinds of music.

People from different cultures have their own **customs**, or ways of doing things. People from China wear red during Chinese New Year for good luck. People from Mexico may have a piñata stuffed with candy treats at a birthday celebration. In Greece, a woman may carry a lump of sugar on her wedding day to make sure she has a sweet life.

 **TextWork**

3 Underline a Mexican custom.

203

❹ How do you contribute to your community?

_____

_____

How We Are Alike

Virginians contribute to their communities in the same ways. They belong to groups. They do their jobs. They follow rules and laws. They take part in community activities. People work together to be responsible citizens.

Although Virginians come from different cultures, they share the same ideas. They believe in the rights of every American citizen. They also share many American traditions. A **tradition** is something that is passed down from older family members to children.

TextWork

5 (Focus Skill) Circle the things we share as Americans.

Family reunions are an American tradition.

Celebrating America

Holidays remind us of our common American traditions. Thanksgiving and Independence Day celebrate our country's history.

September 17 is Constitution Day. It celebrates the signing of the United States Constitution, in 1787.

Some states have their own holidays. Jamestown Landing Day celebrates the day English colonists first came to Virginia.

Saturday
September 17
Constitution Day

Saturday
May 14
Jamestown Landing Day

Celebrating Heroes

Some holidays honor people who have made a difference in American communinties. In January, we honor the work of Dr. Martin Luther King, Jr. In February, we celebrate Presidents' Day. On Memorial Day, in May, we honor those who gave their lives for our country in wars.

 **TextWork**

8 Circle the holiday we celebrate in February.

Monday
May
30
Memorial Day

9 What unites us as Americans?

_____

_____

United We Stand

Americans are united by common principles and traditions. We have a responsibility to be good citizens. We believe that by respecting one another's diversity, we can live and work together in our communities.

Americans sing the national anthem at a baseball game.

1 SUMMARIZE How are people of different ethnic origins and customs united as Americans?

_____

_____

2 What are some American **traditions**?

_____

_____

Circle the letter of the correct answer.

3 Which is an American custom?

    A Singing the national anthem

    B Wearing red on New Year's Day

    C Having a piñata at a birthday party

    D Carrying a lump of sugar

Activity

Research a culture in your community. Then make a bulletin board display of customs from that culture.

It's a Match!

A MARLA FOR MAYOR!
CHOOSE A GOOD LEADER
VOTE FOR MARLA

B MARLA FOR MAYOR!
CHOOSE A GOOD MAYOR
VOTE FOR MARLA

Marla Manning wants to be the city's new mayor. She wants citizens to vote for her in the next election.

Circle the two posters that are exactly alike. Look at the pictures and the words.

Review and Test Prep

The Big Idea

People in communities must follow rules and respect one another's rights.

Summarize the Unit

Focus Skill **Generalize** Fill in the chart with ways to be a responsible citizen.

Facts

Citizens respect the rights and property of others.

_____

_____

_____

_____

_____

_____

Generalization

Responsible citizens help make the community a good place to live, work, and play.

Use Vocabulary

Complete each sentence.

❶ It is my _____ to do my

schoolwork.

❷ People must stop at red lights because it

is the _____.

❸ We have a festival to celebrate the

_____ of all the people in

our community.

❹ I live in a town, and I am a

_____ of my town.

❺ Our class decided the new class pet by

having each person _____

for his or her favorite.

Word Bank

citizen
p. 186

responsibility
p. 186

law
p. 187

vote
p. 194

election
p. 196

diversity
p. 202

Think About It

Circle the letter of the correct answer.

6 How can Martin show self-reliance?

  A Put away his toys when he's finished playing

  B Ask his mother for a glass of water

  C Have his sister help him clean his room

  D Refuse to clean his classroom desk

7 Who makes sure a state's laws are obeyed?

  F Mayor

  G City council

  H Governor

  J City manager

8 Something that is passed down from older family members to children is a—

  A right

  B tradition

  C law

  D rule

9

Mr. Kearney is the mayor of the town. He listens to citizens and works to make the community a better place to live. The citizens elected him to make sure the city's rules and laws are obeyed. Mr. Kearney also suggests new laws.

Which character trait BEST describes Mr. Kearney?

F Self-reliance

G Self-discipline

H Respect

J Trustworthiness

Answer each question in a complete sentence.

10 Why might you choose a trustworthy person as your friend?

_____

_____

11 What are some customs of your culture, and why are they important?

_____

_____

 **Virginia Adventures**

It's my first day on the job as a detective.

Eco Detective Agency

There's a mystery afoot! You and Eco will travel in Virginia and the United States to solve the Case of the Missing Citizen. Play the game now, online or on CD.

HMH

ECO

Show What You Know

Writing Write a Report
Research one of the holidays in this unit. Write a report about the holiday and how it came to be.

Activity Hold an Election
Think of something your class would like to vote on. Make a ballot for each person. Count the votes to see which choice wins.

Vote Here

Great Americans

Spotlight on Standards

THE BIG IDEA Some special Americans have helped make our lives better.

HISTORY AND SOCIAL SCIENCE SOL
2.11

Set the Stage

How have people in the past changed our lives?

Washington, D.C.

"Washington, D.C., was named for our country's first President."

"We remember the people who worked for our freedoms."

"Americans are proud of their country."

219

Preview Vocabulary

freedom

Americans have the **freedom** to follow any religion or none. (page 228)

independence

More than 200 years ago, the United States won its **independence** from England. (page 229)

220

President

President Obama is the leader of the United States. (page 226)

equality

Many Americans have worked for **equality** for all citizens. (page 237)

challenge

African Americans faced the **challenge** of unfair treatment. (page 245)

Focus Skill Cause and Effect

Learn

■ A cause is an event or action that makes something happen.

■ An effect is something that happens because of a cause.

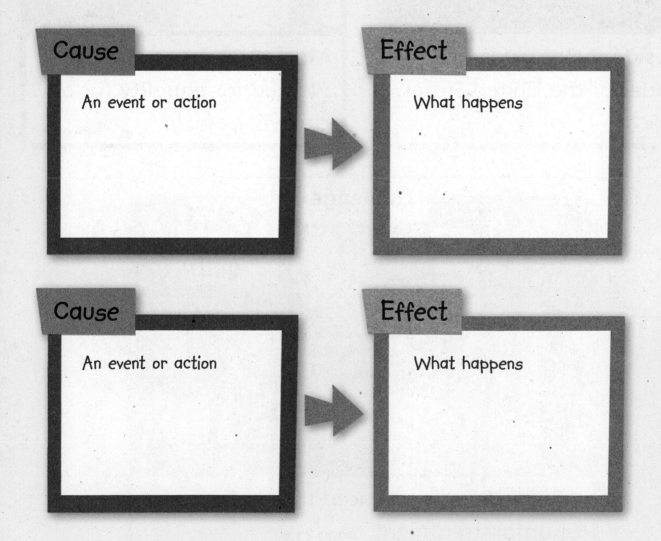

Practice

Read the paragraph below. Underline the effect of Columbus's journey to North America.

Christopher Columbus wanted to find a faster route from Europe to Asia. He sailed across the Atlantic Ocean. Instead of Asia, he landed in North America. Soon, settlers came to live there because of the stories Columbus told.

Cause

Effect

Apply

Read the following paragraph.

People from England started colonies in North America. Because the colonies were ruled by England, the colonists had to obey laws made by England's king. Some colonists thought the laws were unfair. As a result, the colonists decided to form their own country. Thomas Jefferson wrote the Declaration of Independence. It told the king that Americans wanted to be free.

What can you add to the chart about the events that formed America?

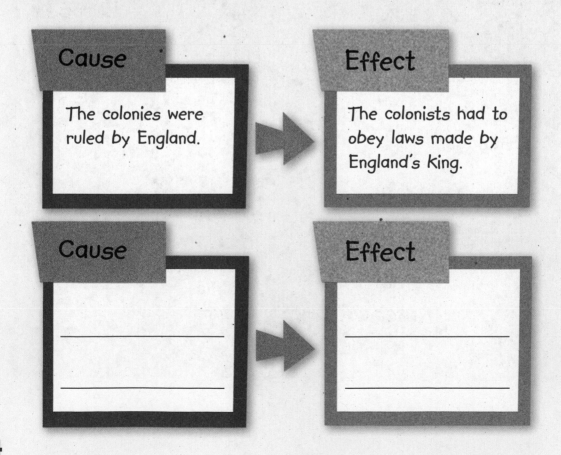

Cause		Effect
The colonies were ruled by England.	→	The colonists had to obey laws made by England's King.

Cause		Effect
_____	→	_____

Two Great Presidents

> Think of some qualities that a good leader must have.

Essential Question

✓ How did George Washington and Abraham Lincoln help to improve the lives of other Americans?

HISTORY AND SOCIAL SCIENCE SOL
2.11

❶ Circle who works in each of the three branches of government.

Our Country's Government

Our country's government has three parts, or branches. Each branch has its own job to do.

Congress makes the laws. The **President** makes sure everyone obeys the laws. The Supreme Court decides if our country's laws are fair to all citizens.

Washington, D.C.

White House

President Barack Obama

226

Washington, D.C.

The leaders of our country meet and work in Washington, D.C. This city is our country's capital. It was named for George Washington, our country's first President.

The Supreme Court and the Capitol building are in Washington, D.C. The White House is also there. The President lives and works in the White House. Leaders from other countries visit the White House to meet with the President.

 TextWork

2 (Focus Skill) Underline the sentence that tells how Washington, D.C., got its name.

3 In the picture, circle where the President lives.

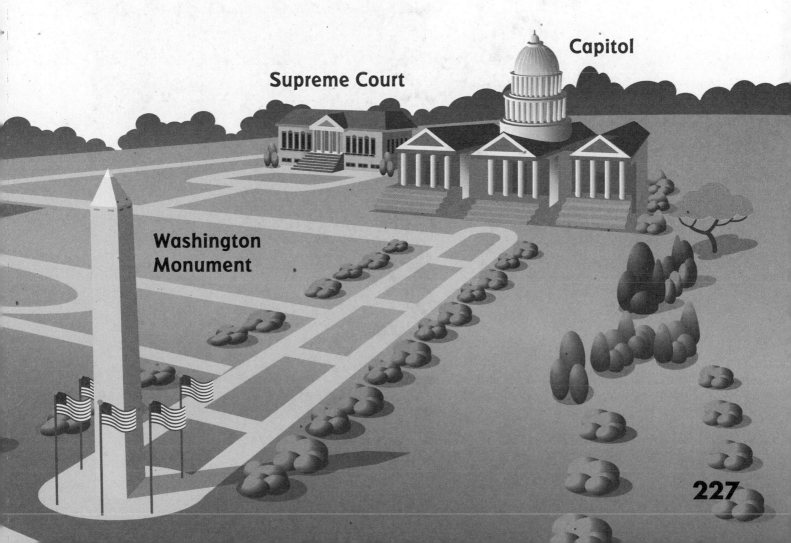

Capitol

Supreme Court

Washington Monument

227

4 Where was George
Washington born?

_____

5 Circle the picture
that shows what
George Washington did
as a young man.

George Washington

George Washington was born in Virginia in 1732. When he was a young man, he worked as a surveyor. He learned how to camp and survive in wild country.

During this time, American colonists grew unhappy with the English government. They wanted to have the freedom to make their own laws. **Freedom** is the right to make choices.

Surveying compass

A surveyor is a person who measures land.

228

The colonists fought a war for independence with England. **Independence** is the freedom of people to choose their own government. This war was called the American Revolution.

George Washington became the leader of the colonists' army. The army was small and its soldiers had little training. Washington used what he learned as a surveyor to help his soldiers.

 **TextWork**

6 (Focus Skill) Underline how George Washington helped the Americans win the war.

George Washington's leadership helped the Americans win the war.

7 Why do you think people wanted George Washington to stay on as President?

_____

_____

Writing the Constitution

In 1787, George Washington worked with other leaders to write a plan for the government of the United States. The plan was called the Constitution.

The American people elected George Washington the first President of the United States. He was President for eight years. Then he retired to his home at Mount Vernon in Virginia.

Mount Vernon

Signing the Constitution

230

Abraham Lincoln

Abraham Lincoln was born in 1809. Seven years later, his family moved to Indiana because the state did not allow slavery. Enslaved people were owned by others and made to work hard without pay. Abraham Lincoln's father felt that this was not right.

Abraham Lincoln did not go to school. He had to work on his family's farm. Still, he learned a lot by reading books he borrowed.

TextWork

8 (Focus Skill) Underline the text that explains why the Lincoln family moved to Indiana.

Abraham Lincoln's birthplace in Kentucky

9 Underline the two groups that fought in the Civil War.

10 Circle the battle that took place the farthest north.

Working to End Slavery

Abraham Lincoln became a lawyer. He was known for being honest and fair. This helped him become President in 1860.

In 1861, the Civil War started. This war was fought between people in two parts of the United States. People in the North and people in the South disagreed about many things. One of them was slavery. President Lincoln tried to keep the country together.

Major Civil War Battles in Virginia

Cedar Creek

Manassas

Wilderness

Chancellorsville   Fredericksburg

Gaines Mill

Appomattox Court House

Petersburg

North

West — East

South

The Civil War was long and hard. Many people on both sides died. The war finally ended in 1865.

The government gave freedom to all enslaved people in the United States. Sadly, President Lincoln was killed five days after the war ended. Today, he is remembered as one of our most important Presidents.

TextWork

❶ How long did the Civil War last?

_____

Lincoln with soldiers

Lincoln Memorial in Washington, D.C.

233

1 **SUMMARIZE** How did George Washington and Abraham Lincoln help to improve the lives of other Americans?

_____

_____

2 How did American colonists win their **independence** from England?

_____

Circle the letter of the correct answer.

3 Where do the leaders of our country meet and work today?

   A Mount Vernon

   B Washington, D.C.

   C Indiana

   D Kentucky

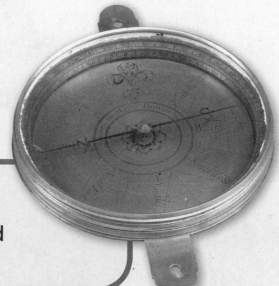

Writing

   Write a report about the ways we honor George Washington and Abraham Lincoln.

Equal Rights for All

Think about some rights that you have.

Essential Question

✓ How did Susan B. Anthony and Dr. Martin Luther King, Jr., help to improve the lives of other Americans?

HISTORY AND SOCIAL SCIENCE SOL
2.11

Working for Equality

During much of our country's history, not all American citizens had the same rights. For many years, women were not allowed to do many things men could do.

Most girls did not go to school for as long as boys did. They could not become doctors or lawyers. Women were paid much less than men were paid for the same work. Women were not allowed to vote.

Women marched for the right to vote.

African Americans were treated unfairly because of the color of their skin. They had to sit at the back of the bus. African American children could not go to the same schools as white children.

Many people worked for **equality**, or equal rights, for all people. Susan B. Anthony helped women win the right to vote. Dr. Martin Luther King, Jr., worked to pass laws that gave African Americans more rights.

2 What does equality mean?

_____

3 Underline the names of two people who helped women and African Americans gain equality.

African Americans were not allowed to eat at some restaurants. They had sit-ins to protest these unfair laws.

Susan B. Anthony

Susan B. Anthony was born in 1820. Her parents taught her that women should have the same choices as men. They also believed that slavery was wrong.

Susan B. Anthony became a teacher. She thought it was unfair that she earned less money than male teachers did. She wanted to help women get the same rights men had.

TextWork

4 (Focus Skill) Circle the reasons Susan B. Anthony worked for equality.

5 Underline a job Susan B. Anthony had.

Susan B. Anthony's birthplace in Massachusetts.

Susan B. Anthony began speaking out against slavery. After slavery was outlawed, she spoke about women's rights. She traveled around the country, giving about 100 speeches each year.

Susan B. Anthony also helped form many groups that worked to give women the right to vote. Although she died in 1906, her work helped women finally win the right to vote, in 1920.

TextWork

6 Underline the two things Susan B. Anthony spoke about.

7 What happened in 1920?

_____

_____

Women voting in New York in the early 1920s

Dr. Martin Luther King, Jr.

Dr. Martin Luther King, Jr., was born in Atlanta, Georgia, in 1929. He became a minister. He spent his life working to make sure African Americans were treated fairly.

In 1963, Dr. King led the March on Washington. There, he made a speech to 200,000 people. This speech, called "I Have a Dream," is one of the most important speeches in American history.

8 What is the name of the speech Dr. King gave in Washington?

_____

_____

240

In 1964, Dr. King won the Nobel Peace Prize for his work. He helped find peaceful ways for people of all colors to get along with one another. That same year, the government passed laws to protect people of all colors. The laws said that people cannot be separated or given fewer rights because of the color of their skin. Today, we honor Dr. King with a national holiday each January.

TextWork

9 Underline the reason Dr. King won the Nobel Peace Prize.

10 On the time line, circle what happened in 1955.

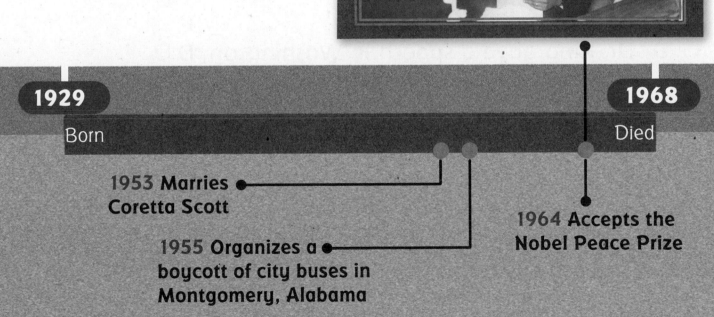

1929
Born

1968
Died

1953 Marries Coretta Scott

1955 Organizes a boycott of city buses in Montgomery, Alabama

1964 Accepts the Nobel Peace Prize

❶ SUMMARIZE How did Susan B. Anthony and Dr. Martin Luther King, Jr., help to improve the lives of other Americans?

_____

_____

❷ How did women work for **equality**?

_____

Circle the letter of the correct answer.

❸ What was the result of Dr. King's work?

   A African Americans won the right to vote.

   B Women won the right to vote.

   C African Americans got equal treatment under the law.

   D Dr. King gave a speech in Washington, D.C.

Activity

Imagine that you are going to take part in the March on Washington. Make a protest sign that you could carry during the march.

Meeting Challenges

Lesson 3

Think of a time in your life when you tried to do something very difficult.

Essential Question

✓ How did Helen Keller and Jackie Robinson help to improve the lives of other Americans?

 HISTORY AND SOCIAL SCIENCE SOL
2.11

243

❶ (Focus Skill) Circle the reason Helen Keller lost her sight and hearing.

❷ What did Anne Sullivan teach Helen to use to communicate?

Helen Keller

Helen Keller was born a healthy baby in 1880. Before she was two years old, she became ill and lost her sight and hearing. She had not yet learned to talk. Now she had no way to communicate.

When Helen was six years old, Anne Sullivan became her teacher. She taught Helen to communicate by using the sense of touch.

Sign language alphabet

w a t e r

Helen Keller and
Anne Sullivan

244

Anne Sullivan formed letters in the palm of Helen's hand. Helen learned to read and write Braille. Braille is an alphabet of raised dots. Helen became the first blind and deaf person to go to college.

Later, Helen Keller spoke to people around the world about the challenges she faced. A **challenge** is a difficulty that needs to be overcome. She also worked with groups that helped people who could not see or hear.

 **TextWork**

3 Underline the text that explains what Braille is.

Helen Keller met many important people, including several Presidents.

Jackie Robinson

Jackie Robinson grew up at a time when people were treated differently because of the color of their skin. He went to college, where he ran track and played football, baseball, and basketball.

He went into the army to serve his country in World War II. He thought that African American soldiers were treated unfairly. He spoke out against this treatment.

TextWork

4 Circle the sports Jackie Robinson played in college.

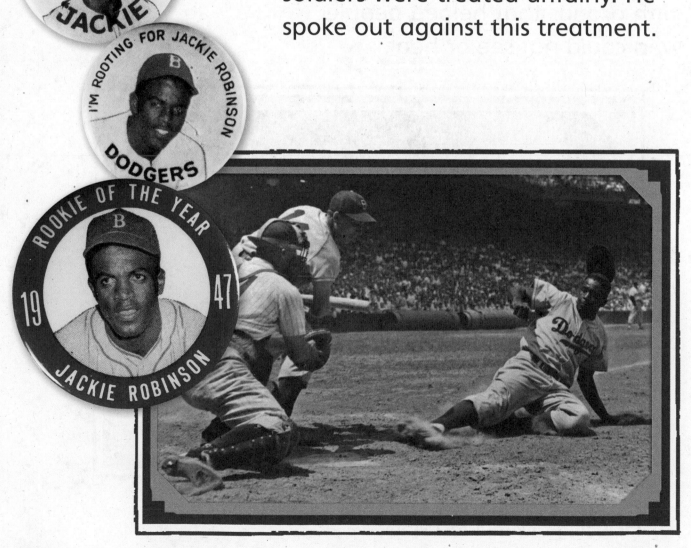

After the army, Jackie Robinson joined the Kansas City Monarchs, an African American baseball team. Then in 1947, he was asked to play for the Brooklyn Dodgers. He was the first African American to play in the major leagues.

At first, some of the other players and fans called him names. Jackie Robinson did not fight back. He let his great baseball playing speak for him.

 TextWork

5 What major league team did Jackie Robinson play for?

_____

Jackie Robinson spoke out for equal rights for all Americans. He was given the Presidential Medal of Freedom for his work.

Good Citizens

Helen Keller and Jackie Robinson were good citizens. Through their actions, they showed others how to overcome the challenges they faced. They also worked to help make the lives of others better.

Many other Americans have worked to make a difference in their communities. You can use your talents and ideas to help people or to make your community a better place.

Good citizens help others.

1 **SUMMARIZE** How did Helen Keller and Jackie Robinson help to improve the lives of other Americans?

_____

_____

2 What **challenges** did Helen Keller face?

_____

_____

Circle the letter of the correct answer.

3 Jackie Robinson helped others by—

   A serving as President of the United States

   B helping blind and deaf people communicate

   C speaking out for equal rights for all Americans

   D helping women win the right to vote

Writing

Write about ways in which you could make a difference in your community.

Good Citizens

Match each citizen with his or her speech.

Martin Luther King, Jr.

Susan B. Anthony

Helen Keller

Abraham Lincoln

> I believe that blind and deaf people can overcome any challenge.

> I have a dream that all people will one day have equal rights.

> I think slavery is wrong.

> I think women should have the right to vote.

Word Search

**Write the word for each definition.
Then circle those words below.**

the leader of our country   _____

the right to make choices   _____

the freedom of people to
choose their own government   _____

equal rights   _____

a difficulty that needs to be
overcome   _____

```
A G N O R S G B L U P C
P U I V E I O N T K H H
R W H F S T C I R Z B A
E D P R O L J S J E Y L
S J L E G Q U L A S X L
I N D E P E N D E N C E
D A V D R A I T E E W N
E X N O B S C Y D M S G
N I F M O L A H I N J E
T A C M O R J Y G U C E
D E Q U A L I T Y A H F
U K U N J M O B H G V O
```

Review and Test Prep

The Big Idea

Some special Americans have helped make our lives better.

Summarize the Unit

(Focus Skill) **Cause and Effect** Fill in the chart to show how Susan B. Anthony and Dr. Martin Luther King, Jr., helped win equal rights for women and African Americans.

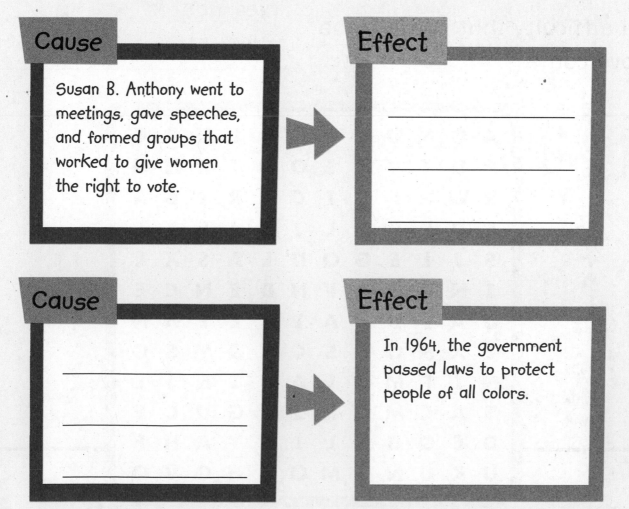

Cause

Susan B. Anthony went to meetings, gave speeches, and formed groups that worked to give women the right to vote.

Effect

_____

_____

_____

Cause

_____

_____

_____

Effect

In 1964, the government passed laws to protect people of all colors.

Use Vocabulary

Write the word that matches the description.

Word Bank

President
p. 226

freedom
p. 228

independence
p. 229

equality
p. 237

Braille
p. 245

challenge
p. 245

1 The leader of our country makes sure everyone obeys the laws.

_____

2 As a young girl, Helen Keller could not communicate with her family.

_____

3 Long ago, leaders in the colonies wanted to be able to make their own laws.

_____

4 We can choose where we want to live and what work we will do.

_____

5 Everyone in the United States has the right to go to school.

_____

Think About It

Circle the letter of the correct answer.

6 George Washington made the lives of Americans better by—

    A freeing all enslaved people

    B helping the colonists win the American Revolution

    C working for equal rights for all Americans

    D giving women the right to vote

7 Who spoke out against slavery and also worked for women's rights?

    F Helen Keller

    G Dr. Martin Luther King, Jr.

    H Jackie Robinson

    J Susan B. Anthony

8 How did Anne Sullivan first help Helen Keller learn to communicate?

    A She helped Helen write a book.

    B She sent Helen to a new school.

    C She formed letters in Helen's hand.

    D She made an alphabet for Helen.

9

Jackie Robinson — baseball player

Both — worked for equal rights for all Americans

Martin Luther King, Jr. — minister

How were Dr. Martin Luther King, Jr., and Jackie Robinson alike?

F Both worked for equal rights.

G Both were ministers.

H Both were baseball players.

J Both worked to stop the vote.

Answer each question in a complete sentence.

10 How do you think life would be different today if women could not vote?

_____

_____

11 Why is the work of Dr. Martin Luther King, Jr., and Susan B. Anthony important?

_____

_____

 **Virginia Adventures**

HALL of LOCAL HEROES

Help me put together the Hall of Heroes exhibit.

The staff at the Time Museum is making a Hall of Heroes exhibit. Do you and Eco know enough about great Americans to help them? Play the game now, online or on CD.

Show What You Know

Writing Write a List
Imagine that Helen Keller is going to be a guest speaker at your school. Write a list of questions you might ask her about overcoming challenges.

Activity Design an Award
To which person from this unit you would like to give an award? Draw a picture of your award and explain your choice.

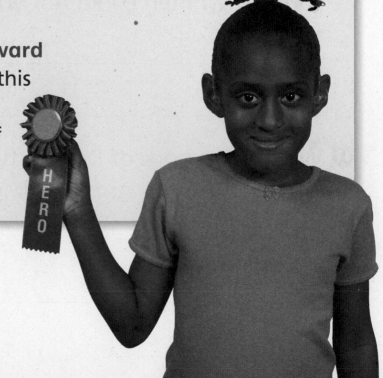

256

For Your Reference

GLOSSARY

INDEX

STANDARDS OF LEARNING

Glossary

The Glossary has important words and their definitions. They are listed in alphabetical (ABC) order. The definition is the meaning of the word. The page number at the end tells you where the word is first used.

adobe
Sun-dried brick made of clay and straw. p. 75

ancestor
A family member who lived long ago. p. 13

ancient
From a time long, long ago. p. 10

architecture
The design of buildings. p. 23

bar graph
A graph that uses bars to show the amounts or numbers of things. p. 115

barter
The exchange of goods and services without the use of money. p. 158

border
A line that shows where a state or a country ends. p. 14

budget
A plan for spending money. p. 168

business
An activity that makes or sells goods or services. p. 160

calendar
A chart of the days, weeks, and months in a year. p. 21

capital
A city in which a state's or a country's leaders meet and work. p. 126

capital resources
Goods made by people and used to produce other goods and services. p. 149

cardinal directions
North, south, east, and west. p. 15

challenge
A difficulty that needs to be overcome. p. 245

citizen
A person who lives in and belongs to a community. p. 186

civilization
A large group of people living in a well-organized way. p. 26

climate
The kind of weather an area has over a long period of time. p. 52

communication
The sharing of ideas and information. p. 111

community
A place where people live, work, and play together. p. 106

compass rose
A symbol that shows direction (north, east, south, and west) on a map. p. 127

consumer
A person who buys and uses goods and services. p. 165

continent
A large body of land on Earth. 11

contribution
The act of giving or doing something. p. 20

country
An area of land with its own people and laws. p. 14

culture
The beliefs, customs, and way of life of a group of people. p. 10

custom
A group's way of doing something. p. 203

dam
A structure built across a river to hold back water. p. 101

desert
A large, dry area of land. p. 14

diversity
Different ideas and ways of living. p. 202

dugout
A boat made from a large, hollowed-out tree trunk. p. 60

election
An event at which people vote for their leaders. p. 196

environment
Surroundings. p. 50

equality

Equal rights. p. 237

equator

An imaginary line around the middle of Earth. p. 118

factory

A building in which people use machines to make things. p. 148

freedom

The right to make choices. p. 228

fuel

A resource, such as oil, that can be burned for heat or energy. p. 147

geography

The study of Earth and the ways people use it. p. 102

globe

A round model of Earth. p. I[I]

goods

Things that can be bought and sold. p. 154

government

A group of citizens that runs a community, state, or country. p. 196

governor

The leader of a state's government. p. 198

hemisphere

A half of Earth. p. 119

history

The study of things that happened in the past. p. 11

honesty

Telling the truth. p. 191

human resources

People working to produce goods and services. p. 148

independence

The freedom people have to choose their own government. p. 229

invention

Something that has not been made before. p. 30

law

A rule that all citizens must follow. p. 187

map

A drawing that shows what places look like from above and where they are located. p. 11

map legend

A list of shapes and symbols used on a map and an explanation of what each stands for. p. 126

map symbol

A small picture or shape that stands for a real thing. p. 15

map title

The name or kind of map. pp. 15, 126

mayor

The leader of a city government or a town government. p. 197

mesa

A flat-topped mountain with steep sides. p. 74

money

Coins, paper bills, and checks used in exchange for goods and services. p. 159

mountain range

A group of mountains. p. 123

natural resources

Materials that come directly from nature. p. 146

ocean

A very large body of salty water. p. 11

plain

A large area of land that is mostly flat. p. 54

pole

One of the two points on Earth farthest from the equator. p. 119

population

The number of people living in a community. p. 107

President

The leader of the United States government. p. 226

producer

A person who uses resources to make goods and/or provide services. p. 164

R

recycle

To use materials in old things to make new things. p. 150

region

An area of land that has common (the same) characteristics. p. 52

responsibility

Something you should take care of or do. p. 186

right

Something people are free to do. p. 188

S

scarcity

Not being able to meet all wants at the same time because resources are limited. p. 166

self-discipline

Thinking about your choices in a calm and careful way. Controlling your temper. p. 190

self-reliance

Doing things for yourself and not asking others to do them for you. p. 190

scribe

A person who records things in writing. p. 22

services

Work done for others for pay. p. 155

state

A part of a country. p. 14

T

technology

New inventions and ideas that make everyday life better. p. 28

teepee

A cone-shaped shelter built by some groups of American Indians. p. 67

tradition

Something that is passed on from older family members to children. p. 205

transportation

A way of moving people and things from one place to another. p. 108

travois

A carrier made by some American Indian groups from a buffalo skin fastened to two poles and usually dragged by a dog. p. 70

trustworthiness

Keeping promises and finishing work that is given to you. p. 191

vote

A choice that gets counted. p. 194

Index

The index tells where information about people, places, and events in this book can be found. The entries are listed in alphabetical order. Each entry tells the pages where you can find the topic.

INDEX

INDEX

◆ Virginia History and Social Science Standards of Learning

History

2.1 The student will explain how the contributions of ancient China and Egypt have influenced the present world in terms of architecture, inventions, the calendar, and written language.

2.2 The student will compare the lives and contributions of three American Indian cultures of the past and present with emphasis on the Powhatan of the Eastern Woodlands, the Lakota of the Plains, and the Pueblo peoples of the Southwest.

2.3 The student will identify and compare changes in community life over time in terms of buildings, jobs, transportation, and population.

Geography

2.4 The student will develop map skills by

  a) locating the United States, China, and Egypt on world maps;

  b) understanding the relationship between the environment and the culture of ancient China and Egypt;

  c) locating the regions of the Powhatan, Lakota, and Pueblo Indians on United States maps;

  d) understanding the relationship between the environment and the culture of the Powhatan, Lakota, and Pueblo Indians.

2.5 The student will develop map skills by

  a) locating the equator, the seven continents, and the five oceans on maps and globes;

  b) locating selected rivers (James River, Mississippi River, Rio Grande, Huang He, Nile River), mountain ranges (Appalachian Mountains and Rocky Mountains), and lakes (Great Lakes) in the United States and other countries.

2.6 The student will demonstrate map skills by constructing simple maps, using title, map legend, and compass rose.

Economics

2.7 The student will describe natural resources (water, soil, wood, and coal), human resources (people at work), and capital resources (machines, tools, and buildings).

2.8 The student will distinguish between the use of barter and the use of money in the exchange for goods and services.

2.9 The student will explain that scarcity (limited resources) requires people to make choices about producing and consuming goods and services.

Civics

2.10 The student will explain the responsibilities of a good citizen, with emphasis on

a) respecting and protecting the rights and property of others;

b) taking part in the voting process when making classroom decisions;

c) describing actions that can improve the school and community;

d) demonstrating self-discipline and self-reliance;

e) practicing honesty and trustworthiness.

2.11 The student will identify George Washington, Abraham Lincoln, Susan B. Anthony, Helen Keller, Jackie Robinson, and Martin Luther King, Jr. as Americans whose contributions improved the lives of other Americans.

2.12 The student will understand that the people of Virginia

a) have state and local government officials who are elected by voters;

b) have diverse ethnic origins, customs, and traditions, who make contributions to their communities, and who are united as Americans by common principles.